P9-EEQ-889

EARLY CHILDHOOD CARE AND EDUCATION
AN INVESTMENT THAT WORKS

By

Shelley L. Smith
Mary Fairchild
Scott Groginsky

National Conference of State Legislatures
William T. Pound, Executive Director

1560 Broadway, Suite 700
Denver, Colorado 80202

444 North Capitol Street, N.W., Suite 515
Washington, D.C. 20001

January 1997

The National Conference of State Legislatures serves the legislators and staffs of the nation's 50 states, its commonwealths, and territories. NCSL was created in January 1975 from the merger of three organizations that served or represented state legislatures. NCSL is a bipartisan organization with three objectives:

- To improve the quality and effectiveness of state legislatures,
- To foster interstate communication and cooperation,
- To ensure states a strong, cohesive voice in the federal system.

The Conference has offices in Denver, Colorado and Washington, D.C.

Photo Credits

Pp. 9 and 19, photos courtesy of the Colorado Children's Campaign's photo library: p. 9, Ray Ng, copyright Ray Ng Photography, used with permission; p. 19, Dennis Schroeder; pp. 31 and 57, Customs House Children's Center, Denver; pp. 41 and 79, Cara Koch, Monday Morning Moms, Colorado Springs, Colo.; p. 49, Downtown Denver Child Care Consortium, Inc.

Printed on recycled paper.

© 1997 by the National Conference of State Legislatures. All rights reserved.
ISBN 1-55516-650-4

Contents

PREFACE AND ACKNOWLEDGMENTS

This second edition of *Early Childhood Care and Education: An Investment That Works* was revised by Shelley Smith and Scott Groginsky. It includes a new chapter seven outlining the child care implications of the new federal welfare reform law. NCSL Children and Family Program staff Dana Reichert and Jack Tweedie contributed significantly to the welfare chapter and Adelia Yee helped with a wide range of research. Other NCSL staff who assisted with the new version include Nina Williams-Mbengue, Barbara Houlik and Steve Christian.

This publication is a product of the Early Childhood Care and Education Project of the National Conference of State Legislatures. The project's primary mission is to provide state legislatures with information and technical assistance on quality early childhood care and education issues.

We are grateful for the support of the Carnegie Corporation of New York, and the Foundation for Child Development, in particular Michael H. Levine, Program Officer for Carnegie, and Susan Blank, Senior Program Associate for the Foundation for Child Development, who have recognized that state lawmakers are instrumental in promoting the importance of early childhood policies.

The authors wish to thank those reviewers who assisted in developing this document. They are not responsible for the final product, but their perspectives undoubtedly improved the document in both content and structure. Specific thanks go to: Helen Blank and Gina Adams, Children's Defense Fund; Susan Blank, Foundation for Child Development; Charles Bruner, Child and Family Policy Center; Mark Greenberg, Center for Law and Social Policy; Debra Hawks, American College of Obstetricians and Gynecologists; Beverly Jackson, National Center for Clinical Infant Programs; Barry Krisberg, National Council on Crime and Delinquency; Joan Lombardi, U.S. Department of Health and Human Services; Bart Lubow, Annie E. Casey Foundation; John Pollak, Iowa Legislative Service Bureau; Larry Schweinhart, High/Scope Educational Research Foundation; Louise Stoney, Stoney Associates; Chantel Walker, National Economic Development and Law Center; and Joni Wall, Louisiana Senate Office of Fiscal Affairs and Policy Development.

NCSL reviewers include: Julie Bell, Education Program Director; Donna Hunzeker, Criminal Justice Program Manager; Martha King, Program Principal, Health Services Program; and Jana Zinser, Senior Policy Specialist, Employment and Job Training.

Executive Summary

Significant economic and social changes over the past two decades have propelled child care and early childhood education to the top of state legislative agendas across the country. Trends include increased global economic competition, a shifting economic base, changing demographics and an influx of mothers into the work force. In addition, an increasing amount of research links early learning experiences with later school achievement, adult productivity and the foundations of a sound future economy. As the United States moves into the 21st century, the demand for competent workers is expected to increase significantly as the actual number of younger workers decreases. Research shows that early childhood education is critical to the nation's future economic position because it provides members of the next generation of workers with a solid foundation of skills, competencies, attitudes and behaviors that will ensure their success in a more technology-based and competitive future economic environment.

As a result of the growing number of working mothers and the increased emphasis on early childhood education, more than half of young children now spend a significant amount of time in child care and prekindergarten programs. Consequently, child care and early childhood education have taken on greater significance across a broad range of policy areas that affect the nation's economic health and well-being.

The implications of state child care and early childhood policies are no longer confined to the traditional domains of human service or education committees. High-quality services for young children have direct implications for achieving a broad range of short- and long-term state policy goals including:

- Allowing welfare recipients to work or train to become self-sufficient;
- Promoting the productivity of the current and future work force;
- Preventing and reducing the incidence of social problems like juvenile violence and delinquency, teen pregnancy, welfare dependence and school failure;
- Preparing young children to succeed in school;
- Facilitating the healthy development of young children; and
- Supporting families by assisting parents in their roles as teachers and nurturers of their children.

> "How individuals function from the pre-school years all the way through adolescence and even adulthood hinges, to a significant extent, on their experiences before the age of three."
>
> —Carnegie Corporation of New York
> *Starting Points: Meeting the Needs of Our Youngest Children*

Recognizing the broad economic implications of child care and early childhood policies, more state legislatures are taking a leadership role in developing early childhood programs. Over the last decade, the number of pieces of early childhood legislation has steadily increased, from approximately 28 in 1984 to 120 in the 1995 legislative sessions. And an increasing number of states are making large investments in programs for young children. In 1994, the states and the **District of Columbia** appropriated over $2.4 billion for early childhood programs. Perhaps the most exciting recent development in state child care and early childhood public policy has been initiatives to integrate state-level efforts across a broad cross-section of social policy goals.

This book presents an in-depth look at how state legislatures are applying the lessons of early childhood research to a broad range of state legislative jurisdictions. It creates a framework for considering early care and education within the context of education, economic development, human services, public health, program regulation and juvenile justice legislative jurisdictions. Separate chapters present the latest relevant program research and outline the range of state legislation related to each of these policy areas. The publication also encourages further cross-jurisdictional consideration of early care and education policies across all these boundaries. This approach is discussed in more depth in the final chapter on family support initiatives.

Early Childhood Care and Education and the Research

The terms "early childhood care and education" denote a variety of services for children from birth through age five and programs for school-age children before and after school and during vacation. For younger children, services encompass child care, day care, nursery school, preschool, prekindergarten, and Head Start. For older children, they include after-school tutorial or recreation programs.

State early care and education programs have developed among three generally separate administrative structures: Head Start programs, prekindergarten and child care subsidies for children receiving public assistance and those of low-income parents. As a federal program, Head Start is administered locally, subject to regulation by the national bureau. Prekindergarten and other programs designed to promote school readiness are often administered through state education departments, and child care subsidy programs most frequently are administered by the state agency responsible for welfare programs. And an increasing number of states have initiated collaborative early childhood and parent education programs that vary in their administrative structures among education, health and human service agencies.

State policymakers can draw on a considerable amount of research data, mostly of two types. First, impact studies look at whether children who participate in early childhood programs are more successful on a variety of measures than their peers without program

experience. The second type of research moved toward identifying program characteristics that produced the positive educational, social and behavioral outcomes for children cited in the impact studies.

The most well-known outcome study of both short- and long-term benefits of early childhood education is the High/Scope Perry Preschool Project. The most recent assessment, when the subjects were 27 years old, concludes that adults born in poverty who attended a high-quality active learning preschool program at ages three and four have fewer criminal arrests, higher earnings and property wealth and greater commitment to marriage than those who did not attend the good preschool. Over participants' lifetimes, an estimated $7.16 is saved for every dollar invested. Educational achievements were significantly different between the two groups with 71 percent vs. 54 percent completing 12th grade or higher. Other significant long-term, outcome research reinforces the High/Scope Perry Preschool findings.

The provider characteristics associated with success are those that lead to a more individualized, attentive and nurturing relationship between the child and the caregiver: smaller group sizes, higher teacher/child ratios and higher staff wages result in quality care. Outcomes for children are also better when they attend programs that include a curriculum geared to young children, well prepared staff and where parents are involved in programming. These characteristics of quality have clear cost implications; however, unless the programs are high-quality, the public and private sector cost-benefits cited in the outcome literature cannot be achieved.

Early Childhood Programs and the Economy

Quality early childhood care and education programs perform a dual function in the economy. In the short run, such services meet the needs of the existing work force by assisting working parents in meeting their child care needs. Research suggests that employers benefit from lower absenteeism and turnover, higher employee morale and reduced recruitment costs by providing child care assistance. In the long term, quality early childhood programs are also critical in preparing children to enter the workplace of the future. Research demonstrates that quality early childhood education programs for at-risk children contribute to higher levels of success in school, greater achievement motivation, higher vocational aspirations and higher employment rates.

Such outcomes, coupled with a changing economic environment, are sparking considerable interest across the states in expanding quality early childhood care and education programs as an economic development strategy. Leading experts indicate that economic growth over the past 20 years has been the result of an influx of people entering the work force, a trend that is not expected to continue. With fewer people entering the labor force, each worker's productivity is critical to achieving a competitive edge in an increasingly global and information-based economy. While educational achievement was less important in a largely manufacturing-based economy, the workplace of the future will demand more critical thinking and learning capacities. Moreover, without tapping the potential of more disadvantaged children, critical labor shortages are expected to stymie economic performance.

The **Oregon** and **Washington** legislatures have responded to the early childhood program research by linking service expansion with broader economic development initiatives. In **Oregon**, early childhood policy was integrated with a larger, economic development and state restructuring package. **Washington's** initiative focused more narrowly on initiating and expanding an early care and education program. The **Oregon** legislature enacted a unique comprehensive system of outcome measures—called benchmarks—to guide the direction of all state government. Within this large-scale, results-oriented strategy, high priority is given to early childhood education. In **Washington**, a comprehensive preschool program for at-risk four-year-olds was created and expanded primarily as a specific economic development strategy.

To support the current work force with their child care needs, state legislatures have launched a number of initiatives. Among the most common are loan and grant programs to increase supply, corporate tax incentives to encourage private child care initiatives on the part of employers, personnel policy requirements for state workers and others to encourage "family-friendly" work environments, support of information and referral services to assist parents as child care consumers, and space allocation policies requiring or providing incentives for developers to plan for child care services. In **Maine**,

the 1993 legislature garnered significant state business support for a comprehensive initiative to increase the supply of affordable quality child care services for low-income parents.

Early Care and Education and the Schools

Today, young people have a distinct and growing need to think creatively, adapt their learning and perform academically. For future generations, success depends on the capacity to function in an increasingly competitive and technology-based global economy. America can no longer afford increasing numbers of children unprepared to learn, high dropout rates or graduates who enter the work force without basic and adaptable skills. Research suggests that the foundation for academic success is laid well before a child enters the public schools. These data indicate that a child's early years are crucial to brain development and academic achievement. As a result, state policy attention is being directed to quality early childhood education services—programs that have repeatedly been shown to increase children's prospects for future school accomplishments. Among legislatures concerned about promoting school readiness, early childhood education is increasingly a preferred policy option. **Georgia, Kentucky** and **Ohio** offer examples of states that have invested heavily in early care programs.

Besides prekindergarten initiatives, lawmakers also are addressing new ways of using the public schools to help students achieve their full academic potential. State lawmakers are exploring ways to use the public education system to meet family and social services needs through school-linked or -based social services programs.

Early Care and Education and Juvenile Justice

Juvenile justice issues are at the top of state legislative agendas across the country. In the last two legislative sessions, 49 states and the **District of Columbia** together passed at least 617 juvenile justice enactments. This legislative activity reflects primarily "get tough" approaches to address perceptions of rampant juvenile violence. Although overall juvenile arrests are relatively stable, arrests for violent offenses rose consistently during the past decade, especially for murder and aggravated assaults. Though youth violence is only part of general violent crime trends, state legislators and their constituents are legitimately concerned about the growing proportion of violent juvenile offenders. Barring more effective interventions, demographics suggest that juvenile violence is likely to increase, rather than subside.

Research suggests that punishment-oriented responses, resulting in longer incarceration or secure confinement, have not reduced juvenile delinquency and are very expensive. By contrast, research points to promising prevention efforts that are more cost-effective in the long-term. One such approach involves quality early childhood services, which can lead to fewer arrests and less violent behavior later in life. A cost-benefit analysis of the High/Scope Perry Preschool Program study, for example, found that quality preschool reduces the costs of crime by nearly $150,000 per program participant over a lifetime. Further, researchers find that certain prevention programs mitigate some of the primary and interrelated risk factors that have been associated with delinquency and crime. For example, studies show home-visiting programs for at-risk families with infants reduce a known risk factor: child abuse. Armed with these important research findings, some legislatures are turning to quality early childhood care and education intervention as a strategy to prevent juvenile violence and delinquency. Most recently, lawmakers in **Tennessee**, **North Carolina** and **Washington** have incorporated early childhood and other prevention programs as a central strategy in their violence prevention packages.

Early Care and Education and Public Health

Good health care, nutrition and environment influence human development from conception into adulthood. A considerable body of research attests to the cost-benefits of adequate primary care and preventive medicine—particularly during pregnancy and in children's early years. A variety of studies confirm the cost-benefits of immunization programs for young children and adequate prenatal care to prevent low birthweight.

Research also confirms that the influence of early environment on brain development is long-lasting. One study followed two groups of inner-city children; the first group was exposed, from infancy to good nutrition, toys and playmates; the second was raised in less stimulating

settings. The study showed that the positive factors had a measurable effect on brain function at age 12 years, and the impact was even greater by age 15. This research suggests that over time the benefits of early intervention are cumulative and confirms the importance of both health and caregiving on child development.

Fifty-three percent of mothers now return to work within a year of a child's birth, and welfare policies increasingly call on mothers of young children to join the labor force as soon as possible. Thus, public policies around the quality of care and health care programming provided for infants and young children take on greater significance. Successful child development depends on the environment in which a child spends his or her time, and for increasing numbers of infants and toddlers, this place is a child care setting for much of the day.

States are beginning to address health components of child care programs in a variety of ways. To date, the bulk of activity involves interagency agreements to coordinate public health services with the early care and education infrastructure. Most often, linkages are established among Medicaid, state public health programs, Maternal and Child Health Services, the Women, Infants and Children's Nutrition Program, and Head Start or other child care programs to coordinate prenatal, postnatal, well-baby care, child health screening, nutrition and parent education programs.

In some states, legislatures have linked health and early care needs by including health requirements in mandates for state-funded preschool programs. In **Ohio** and **Oregon**, state program requirements resemble those of federal Head Start services in terms of their comprehensive health components. In at least 13 other states, legislation requires certain early care and education providers to ensure that children are immunized. Although state legislatures are just beginning to address the linkages between health and child care services, such efforts are likely to expand with the increasing recognition of the importance of adequate health care as a critical determinant of a child's development.

Early Care and Education and Program Regulation

Studies show that the quality of early childhood care and education is inadequate in many cases. This is troubling, because quality is the key determinant in whether the experience will provide positive outcomes for children. Research informs us that caregiving relationships in child care settings affect children's social development, language development and cognitive skills. When there are too many children in a group or too few child care workers per child, learning and classroom involvement suffer. One way state legislatures advance higher quality services is by developing and enforcing regulations, such as improving professional standards for providers or staff/child ratios. While conscious of overregulation, legislators have the pivotal role in program oversight and are recognizing the connection between state regulatory environments and outcomes for children. Other regulatory areas that legislators are addressing are staff wages, screening providers for criminal and child abuse history, and smoking in child care facilities.

Early Childhood Services and Welfare Reform

Enacted in 1996, new federal welfare law requires major restructuring of states' welfare programs and expansion of states' child care services. Under the Temporary Assistance for Needy Families (TANF) program, the federal guarantee of cash assistance for the nation's poor families and children begun during the New Deal of the 1930s is abolished. Instead the new legislation allows time limited federal assistance to individuals through a block grant to the states. The legislation ends the federal entitlement to child care established under the 1988 Family Support Act for working welfare recipients, those in work and training programs, and—in the first twelve months—those who leave welfare for work. Again, the Congress opted for a new six-year block grant to the states for child care services for TANF participants. The legislation consolidates four federal child care funding streams, increases initial allocations above expected funding under the previous system, and requires administration by the state agency responsible for the Child Care and Development Block Grant (CCDBG) of 1990.

Under the welfare legislation, states must meet stringent new work participation requirements that rise rapidly to include 50% of a state's adult TANF population within six years or lose part of their block grant. These new work obligations will increase the demand for child care in the states dramatically. States have considerable flexibility in fashioning child care programs to meet new demands, but—in the long term—they will be doing so with fewer federal reaources available to them than under the old system. Although states initially receive more money compared to prior years, as work requirements and child care demand rise, the federal share under the block grant is set rather than rising with need as in an open-ended entitlement.

At the same time, the integration of federal funding streams offers a significant opportunity for states to streamline and consolidate child care services under one administrative structure. It removes federal barriers to more efficient administration of child care funding streams that in the past had separate rules and regulations. Their integration under the CCDBG paves the way for state consolidation and potential administrative savings. And the demands precipitated by the law create new incentives to better coordinate welfare-related child care programs with state preschool and Head Start services to maximize reaources for the influx of welfare recipients with new work obligations.

State lawmakers are pivotal in the successful implementation of P.L. 104-193 since legislatures must appropriate the new funds and make a variety of related policy choices. Crafting an effective state welfare strategy, however, should encompass policy goals related to both parents and their children. Children from welfare families are at higher risk for academic failure and other negative outcomes that can be remediated by enriched early care and education programs. Under federal welfare reform, state legislatures face critical new responsibilities in assuring that child care services are both available to maintain families' transition to the work force and of sufficient quality to promote school-readiness and healthy outcomes for children from welfare families. **Illinois, Iowa, Utah,** and **Florida** are among states that have developed policies to expand child care options or promote quality as part of their welfare reform stategies.

Early Care and Education and Family Support

Families today face unprecedented challenges in raising their youngsters. Low earnings require many families to resort to multiple wage-earners, moonlighting and overtime, leaving them less time for their families. Real wages have declined disproportionately for younger, less experienced workers and even more for less educated workers.

Growing numbers of young parents resort to extraordinary measures to make ends meet and arrange their child care. Concern about balancing work and family life is not confined to those with low incomes: fully half the population report that they have too little time for their families. And few workplaces offer "family-friendly" policies to help parents balance work and family responsibilities. Parents also are concerned about the quality of child care that they can afford, and indeed a recent study rated most care for infants and toddlers as barely adequate or inadequate.

In an attempt to respond more adequately to changing family needs, legislatures are experimenting with multigenerational family support and education programs. In contrast to traditional services that focus on crisis intervention and strict eligibility requirements, family support approaches build on family strengths by helping parents improve their capacity to be nurturing and to cope with day-to-day stresses. Programs often combine a specific emphasis on parent education and skill-building with better linkages to concrete services like early care and education or job training. Programs vary in setting, format and emphasis, but all share a focus on meeting family-defined needs flexibly.

Legislatures across the country have funded a variety of early intervention, parent education and other types of family support services. Many programs have shown considerable promise in achieving specific outcomes—assisting parents in their familial roles, reducing the incidence of child abuse and neglect, improving school readiness and improving maternal and child health. Among the most well-known initiatives are **Hawaii**'s Healthy Start, **Maryland**'s Friends of the Family, **Missouri**'s Parents as Teachers and **Kentucky**'s Family Resource and Youth Service Centers. In **North Carolina**

and **West Virginia** comprehensive family support initiatives are currently under way through partnerships between the executive and legislative branches of government. These initiatives are unique in their recognition of the role of early childhood services in broader family support reform movements.

Although many family support initiatives have shown great promise in achieving better outcomes for families, significant barriers exist to their application on a broad scale. Federal and state funding streams continue to favor crisis intervention, rather than prevention. State agencies and special interests also often resist change and even well-meaning experts disagree about the most appropriate reform vehicles. Legislative institutions are also part of the problem since in most of them no one committee considers all policies related to children and their families. Instead, particular aspects of family issues are relegated to a variety of jurisdictions that include economic development, labor, education, judiciary, regulation, human services and fiscal committees. Some legislatures have created new structures or processes in an attempt to handle family issues more holistically. **Tennessee**'s Joint Select Committee on Children and Youth, for example, has been particularly effective in providing a vehicle for cross-jurisdictional consideration of family support policies.

Conclusion

This publication highlights recent legislative efforts to expand early care and education, promote the development of young children, and meet a wide variety of state policy goals. Among the expanded policy goals are economic development and education, juvenile violence prevention and welfare reform. In the future, such pioneering state initiatives to support children and their families will increasingly be viewed as complementary elements of a broad approach to state policy development that empowers families to provide the productive and self-sufficient citizens of today and tomorrow.

CHAPTER I

THE ROLE OF EARLY CHILDHOOD CARE AND EDUCATION IN STATE PUBLIC POLICY

Introduction

Our children are the foundation of the future. What happens to children in their early years will echo throughout the coming decades. If they receive a solid foundation, children will develop into stable, contributing members of society. If their care is lacking, the effects will be seen in all parts of society—in families, schools, the economy, and the public health, welfare, and criminal justice systems.

In today's society, more than half of young children spend a great deal of time during their early, formative years outside the family in a variety of child care and early education settings. Well-documented research indicates that these settings, if of high quality, can

- prepare the future workforce to succeed in school and gain skills needed to compete in a global economy;
- enable millions of parents of young children to work productively outside the home;
- allow welfare recipients to work or train to become self-sufficient;
- prevent social problems such as juvenile violence and delinquency, teen-age pregnancy, welfare dependence, and school failure; and
- strengthen families.

In recognition of the importance of early childhood services, state legislatures are enacting related legislation. Over the past decade, the number of pieces of early childhood legislation has steadily expanded—from 28 in 1984 to 120 in the 1995

legislative sessions. In addition, states have made large investments in early childhood programs. In fiscal year 1994, the 50 states and the **District of Columbia** invested nearly $2.4 billion on direct service expenditures for early childhood care and education.[1]

In many states, early childhood services have become an integral component of a much broader public policy debate. An increasing number of states no longer confine consideration of childhood policy to human services and education committees. In some cases, early care issues also are being considered in economic development or juvenile justice committees. In other states, early care is considered in children, youth and

It is more evident today than ever before that the experiences of young children during their early years shape the problems and challenges in public policy that adults are called upon to solve.

families committees with broad jurisdiction over a number of policy areas related to children and their families. Legislators are becoming aware of the importance of creating institutional linkages within the legislative process to address the multifaceted aspects of early childhood development. Within this context, policymakers from fiscal, criminal justice, economic development, and health committees have an important role to play in developing early childhood policies.

For the most part, however, early care and education policies are still viewed narrowly within most state legislatures. Most programs initiated by state legislatures operate on a small scale and are designed to meet limited objectives. This publication is designed to help legislative institutions further examine the cross-jurisdictional impact of state early childhood care and education policies. While early care and education has traditionally been handled by either education or human services legislative jurisdictions, the impact of quality early care programs extends well beyond these conventional policy boundaries. This book creates a framework for considering early care and education from the perspective of a broad range of public policy jurisdictions including the economy, education, welfare, juvenile justice, health and family support.

The Value of a Cross-Jurisdictional Approach

Why a cross-jurisdictional approach? Because, it is more evident today than ever before that the experiences of children during their early years shape the problems and challenges in public policy that adults are called upon to solve. Furthermore, more integrated policy approaches are necessary to improve and expand services within reasonable state budget parameters. This is particularly important as applied to public programs for the most needy—to children who are at risk and who demand significant commitments from the public sector.

The good news is that there now exists a significant research foundation to inform state policy development. Today, lawmakers know with great confidence not just that quality programs work, but also what makes them work. Furthermore, the lessons of early childhood research can be applied across a broad range of larger policy debates that cut across jurisdictional boundaries to include economic development, education, welfare reform, juvenile justice, health, program regulation and

family support issues. In particular, well-documented research indicates that early childhood services contribute to the foundation for a strong economy, a world-class education system and support a key thread in our nation's social fabric: the family.

This book has a two-fold purpose. First, it seeks to educate a diverse cadre of lawmakers from separate jurisdictions about early care and education to inform decisionmaking within their particular areas of expertise. Second, it encourages further cross-jurisdictional consideration of early care and education policies. This approach recognizes the reality of the legislative process: it is both incremental and developmental; that is, without progressive advances in understanding the role of early care and education within separate policy areas, cross-cutting comprehensive approaches are unlikely. As knowledge of the broad policy implications of early care and education grows within each committee however, so will examples of integrated, cross-jurisdictional state policy approaches.

This chapter presents the rationale for policymakers to take a closer look at early care and education both within and beyond their own policy fields. It defines the three major early care and education service systems and presents an overview of the relevant research. Most important, it emphasizes the critical role of quality programming in achieving positive outcomes for children that, in turn, affect policy areas discussed in subsequent chapters. Quality considerations are also discussed in great depth in chapter 6, which covers child care regulatory policies, a domain that crosses a variety of legislative jurisdictions.

Subsequent chapters present the best information to date about the effect of early care and education policy on education, economic development, welfare reform, health, program regulation, juvenile justice and family support. Each chapter (1) addresses the rationale for considering early childhood services in a seemingly different policy debate and (2) provides examples of actual state legislative approaches that integrate early childhood services within each committee jurisdiction.

The chapter topics correspond with common patterns of state legislative organization and committee structures. This format is designed to assist legislators who sit on children's committees and on other influential committees that do not traditionally address children's issues or who have less information about the relevance of early care and education policies to their specific jurisdictions. At the same time, the book encourages legislators to apply early care issues across jurisdictional boundaries. Such comprehensive approaches are discussed in greatest depth in the concluding chapter on the role of early care and education in broad-based family support initiatives.

Early Care and Education Services

Child care is no longer thought of as separate from learning. Instead, care and education of young children are simultaneous—children learn in all settings. High-quality programs address two policy objectives. They provide safe environments that allow parents to work without worrying about their children. At the same time, these programs can provide stimulating and nurturing settings that foster healthy child development, prepare children to succeed in school and give them the tools they need to develop into productive adults.

The term "childhood care and education services" means all types of education and care for children from birth through age five and programs for school-age children before and after school and during vacation.[2] For younger children, this includes child care, day care, nursery school, pre-school, pre-kindergarten and Head Start. For older children, this includes after-school tutorial or recreation programs.

Good programs, however, involve more than a program title. According to the research, quality programming for young children is the key to achieving positive outcomes for individual children and to affecting other areas of public policy. In other words, without a quality program, the improved results promised in the most well-known research are not assured.

Just as state early care and education policy development frequently occurs within certain traditional committee jurisdictions, no one administrative structure retains responsibility for program management. State early care and education programs have developed among three generally separate administrative structures. These include Head Start programs, pre-kindergarten and child care subsidies for children receiving public assistance and those whose parents have low incomes.[3]

As a federal program, Head Start is administered locally, subject to regulation by the national bureau. Prekindergarten and other programs designed to promote school readiness are often administered through state education departments, while child care subsidy programs most frequently are administered by the state agency responsible for welfare programs. Additionally, an increasing number of states have developed parent education and early childhood programs with the public purpose of supporting parents in meeting the needs of their children. Administration of these programs varies from state to state among education, health and human service agencies. Thus, in assessing state programs, lawmakers must be familiar with a collection of services with varying purposes, administered by a variety of agencies.

Head Start

Head Start, launched in 1965, is designed to break the cycle of poverty by providing preschool children from low-income families with a comprehensive program to meet their emotional, social, health, educational and psychological needs. In addition to early childhood education services, Head Start provides a comprehensive health care program, including medical, dental, mental health and nutritional services. Social service staff are available to provide referrals and emergency assistance to families, as well as support services for children with special needs. To ensure that the educational program reflects the cultural and ethnic characteristics of the community, members of the community to be served by a Head Start

WHAT ARE EARLY CHILDHOOD SERVICES?

"Early childhood services" refers to a wide range of programs in different settings. For example:

- The child care services that allow a mother with young children to hold down a job.

- The Head Start program that prepares a child trapped in poverty to succeed in first grade.

- The preschool program that prevents a young boy's later involvement in gang activities.

program must be an integral part of the program's staff (including bilingual staff when necessary).

Perhaps the most unique characteristic of Head Start is its commitment to parent empowerment, which begins with shared decisionmaking in all aspects of the program, including management decisions, fundraising, community outreach and education. Head Start has been very successful in helping parents enter the workforce as employees of the program. Using the Child Development Associate (CDA) program to train, assess and credential caregivers, Head Start has been able to train parents to become professionals in the child care field.

Although the Head Start program has been very successful, some criticize it for failing to meet the growing demand for full-time child care for employed, low-income families. The reasons for this are two-fold. First, most Head Start programs operate for only a few hours a day or only a few days a week. Only an estimated 6 percent of the nation's Head Start children are enrolled in programs that operate at least nine hours a day—the extended hours necessary to serve families who are employed full time. Second, the Head Start income eligibility ceiling, which caps eligibility at the federal poverty level (currently $15,455 for a family of four), makes the program unavailable to many employed, low-income families. At the national level, efforts are under way to address some of these issues. The 1994 program reauthorization, for example, encourages local programs to meet the full-day, full-year service needs of certain families and strengthens collaborative efforts between Head Start and other early childhood service providers.

Prekindergarten Programs

Building on the success of Head Start, many state legislatures have elected to establish state-funded prekindergarten programs. Most typically, these programs target children from low-income families and provide part-day early childhood education services (2 1/2 to three hours in length) during the school year. Some states have established programs for the full school day (generally

8 a.m. to 3 p.m.) or programs that are more universally available. Traditionally, prekindergarten programs have been administered by local school districts, although some states permit the schools to contract with a Head Start or community-based child care program to provide services either in or near the school. More recently, state prekindergarten programs are awarded on a competitive basis to schools, Head Start Programs or other local child care providers. These exciting new initiatives are designed to build on the existing community-based early care and education infrastructure within local communities.

EARLY CARE AND EDUCATION PROGRAMS IN THE STATES

In some states, legislatures have invested in large-scale or comprehensive early care and education programs. For example, the **North Carolina** legislature recently appropriated $67.4 million for its Smart Start early childhood program for fiscal year 1997. The **Ohio** legislature appropriated $145.6 million for fiscal years 1996 and 1997 to supplement federal Head Start programs within the state. **Hawaii** invests around $15 million annually for its after-school programs. And **Washington** has increased its spending on preschool programs for at-risk four-year-olds over nine-fold since 1986 and currently spends $28.3 million annually on the program.

Because of their strong links to the public school system, many state prekindergarten programs require that classes be taught by certified teachers and emphasize the use of a developmentally appropriate curriculum. Traditionally, state prekindergarten programs with a primary education focus seldom include the other family support services such as social, health, nutrition and parent involvement services to meet Head Start performance standards. Newer initiatives are more comprehensive and often include other components in a effort to better meet education goals.

Child Care Subsidies

A variety of funding streams have been created by federal, state and local governments to help low-income families pay for child care while they work or attend training or education. In most states these funds are administered by the Department of Social Services, or its designee, although a few states administer these funds through the Education

Department or another state agency. Many states have also chosen to contract with community-based organizations to administer the funds on the local level.

Child care subsidies may be administered in several ways, including contracts with child care centers in specific low-income neighborhoods, vouchers that may be used in a variety of early childhood programs or for home-based child care, or cash reimbursement or advances directly to parents.

Issues in Coordinating Systems

Although the three primary service systems traditionally have developed with different administrative structures and funding streams to achieve separate goals, they also may be used in coordination with one another to meet broader policy purposes. Many states are experimenting with "wrap-around" or "collaborative" initiatives that attempt to use funds from a variety of sources to provide enriched developmental programming for low-income children while at the same time providing full-day child care services for their parents. Although these collaborative efforts can be successful, some formidable barriers exist to implementing dual-purpose programs on an institutional level:

- **The various components of the early childhood care and education "system" often lack respect and understanding of one another.** School-based prekindergarten programs and administrators often perceive community-based child care programs as providing lesser quality care. Head Start staff often decry early childhood programs that are not evaluated on the basis of Head Start performance standards. Center-based child care programs frequently question the quality of care provided in home-based programs. Child care programs often question the lack of consideration for parents' needs for full-day care within Head Start or state prekindergarten programs. It is important to note, however, that research does not support the belief that quality varies systematically by type of setting.

- **The many federal, state and local laws, rules and regulations with which early childhood programs must comply are often inconsistent and, at times, even conflict.** The plethora of regulations makes it nearly impossible to coordinate funding streams in some circumstances.

- **Different state and federal agencies are responsible for overseeing the administration of the various early childhood care and education funding streams.** State departments of social services and education often find it difficult to coordinate administration of early childhood funds. Additionally, state legislatures and administrators generally have no authority over how Head Start funds are allocated, making it difficult for them to coordinate funds at the state level or target services to specific populations or communities.

- **Early childhood providers who attempt to combine funds from multiple sources are often caught in the difficult situation of responding to multiple administrative agencies with different accountability measures, data collection needs and reporting requirements.** In addition to struggling with the complexity of responding to multiple funders, program directors often fear that their efforts to combine funds to support the cost of full-day services will be seen as "double dipping."

Overview of the Research

In addressing state early care and education policies— both within committee jurisdictions and across them—a considerable amount of research data is now available to state policymakers. The most rigorous and reliable research over the past three decades falls into two categories. In the first—commonly called impact studies—researchers attempt to determine whether children who participate in early care programs are more or less successful than their peers without program experience on a variety of measures. The second type of research grew out of successful impact studies: researchers moved toward identifying program characteristics that produced the positive outcomes for children cited in the impact studies. In other words, research focused on what determines program quality.[4]

Although major research in each area will be discussed separately, outcome and quality research are inseparable. Well-documented research shows that quality early childhood care can influence human development and behavior from childhood through adolescence into adulthood. And these outcomes can affect a wide variety of public policy areas, ranging from

WHAT IS A QUALITY EARLY CHILDHOOD PROGRAM?

A growing research base has defined factors that produce quality early childhood care and education programs. Many factors reflect common sense. For example, research shows that when providers have fewer children to care for they can provide each with more individual attention. In addition, providers who are better paid and who have adequate benefits are more likely to have greater enthusiasm about their work and to stay on the job. Important components of quality include the following:

1. **Well-prepared and well-compensated providers**
- Workers are trained and educated about how children grow and develop, how to respond to their unique temperaments and how to understand a child's rate of physical and emotional growth.
- Workers are warm, friendly, respectful, affectionate and sensitive toward the children in their care; they listen and talk with them, help them with their feelings and apply consistent but flexible rules.
- Workers' expectations vary appropriately for children of differing ages and interests.
- Workers receive satisfactory staff pay and benefits. This leads to reduced turnover, a stabilizing element for children.

2. **A few children for each provider**
- Small group size promotes less hostile and disruptive behavior among children.
- Workers with fewer children can provide more individualized attention and interaction.

3. **Parent involvement**
- Parents are welcome to observe, discuss and recommend policies, and participate in the program's activities.
- Workers share children's experiences with parents and are alert to family needs.
- Workers respect families' varying cultures and backgrounds.

4. **Links to comprehensive community services**
- Programs have access to a broad range of services, including health.
- Workers refer families to other appropriate agencies, such as health care, parent education or counseling.

5. **A safe, healthy, comfortable environment**
- Curriculum is appropriate and balanced and includes individual and group activities and experiences that promote independent thinking, along with physical, emotional and social growth.
- Adequate materials, such as climbing equipment, toys that stimulate creativity and books appropriate to each child's age.
- Safe furnishings.
- Strong hygiene policies.

education and economic development to crime and welfare prevention. But without a quality program these returns on public sector investment will not be achieved.

Outcome Research
The High/Scope Perry Preschool Project. The most well-known outcome research on early care for children is the High/Scope Perry Preschool Project. At the time the study began no evidence "even suggested that a preschool program for children three- and four-years-old could set in motion a chain of events leading to such lifetime effects on children."[5] These lifetime effects have a direct impact on public policy within multiple jurisdictions.

To date, this project has conducted the most comprehensive, longitudinal study of any comparable program. Essentially, the project has tracked 123 children born in poverty and at risk of failing in school for almost 30 years. Under a strictly controlled experimental design, children were initially assigned to a program group and a nonprogram group. Children in the program group were enrolled in a high-quality, active learning preschool program that used a specific, developmental curriculum. Regular home visits and other forms of parental involvement were also significant features of the program. The nonprogram children did not participate in a preschool program.

Findings from the most recent research on the project show positive lifetime effects on the program group and ultimately on the public sector. The research links a range of positive outcomes from the time the child enters school through adulthood with participation in the High/Scope Perry Preschool Program. Specifically, a child's participation sets in motion a chain of child behavior and classroom events that help children avoid assignment to special education and lead to higher levels of school completion and to better out-of-school adjustment, which in turn translates to adult, real-world success. Compared with nonprogram group adults, program-group adults obtain better jobs, have more income, commit to home ownership and engage in family formation within marriage. One group of researchers reported that "crime—with its cycle of drugs, arrests, sentences and difficult relations with civil authorities—is reduced; and welfare usage, with its accompanying patterns of dependency and single parenthood, is tempered."[6]

This description of results illustrates the snowball effect of quality early care for young children. It cannot be emphasized enough, however, that the success of the High/Scope Perry Preschool Project graduates is due to their participation in a program of high quality. In its curriculum, quality is characterized by emphasis on active learning and child-initiated experiences. Using this curriculum encourages "the development of dispositions that support the development of school skills and thus leads to better learning and social behavior."[7] It is this experience that results in later successes and reduced social costs. One thing leads to another: quality preschool experience leads to increased success in school, fewer school dropouts, more employed adults and less criminal behavior. Remarkably, the results of the preschool years link directly to the working adult's social adjustment and productivity.

Research on academic outcomes. Other significant long-term, outcome research reinforces the Perry Preschool findings, particularly with respect to improved academic outcomes. At least 11 additional studies have documented improved outcomes for children in quality early childhood programs. Most of these studies measured performance on intelligence tests and school achievement. Although IQ measures generally show an immediate boost in scores for children who experience preschool intervention, these results tended to dissipate over time.

Although researchers were initially discouraged by the discovery of this "fade-out" effect on IQ gains, in most cases children who had participated in early care and education programs continued to outperform their peers on other important outcome measures. These include school achievement tests, grade-point average, passing to the next grade level and reduced placement in special education.[8] High/Scope researchers also report that there is virtually no evidence of fade-out with respect to measures of delinquency.[9] This suggests that, regardless of IQ measures, participation in a quality program produces consequential benefits for both individual children and society at large.

Research on parental involvement. Another area of research with implications for state policy relates to studies of programs that focus on both parents and children. Although many successful programs—including the High/Scope Perry Preschool Project—include an extensive parental involvement component that is considered crucial to program effectiveness, newer research focuses on child development programs like Missouri's Parents As Teachers Program with a more specific focus on supporting parents in promoting their children's development. (A variety of these programs are discussed in more detail in chapter 8.) One review of the research concludes:

The evidence from a selection of the best designed family-oriented early childhood intervention studies of the past 25 years suggests that these programs can produce positive short- and long-term effects. Most of the long-term evidence relates to more successful school careers for program children and better social adjustment in school and community. But there is also a growing, albeit still modest, body of data pointing to an improved life course for mothers involved in these programs and better long-term parent-child relationships. In other words, these programs may be uniquely suited to reach and to alter the likely life course of two generations. Effects on parent and child may even reinforce each other over time.[10]

Research on Quality

In reviewing the literature, it is evident that achieving better outcomes for children is no accident. Certain programmatic and provider characteristics are associated with success in early care and education programs (see box on page 6). Chief among them are factors that affect a more indiviualized and nurturing relationship between child and caregiver. The 1995 study, Cost, Quality and Child Outcomes in Child Care Centers, for example, found that high teacher/child ratios are the most statistically significant factor that affects quality of programs.[11] Other studies have corroborated these findings. One, commissioned by the **California** Legislature, examined the impact of increasing the number of children per teacher. Researchers found evidence of declining program quality as teachers assumed responsibility for more children. Clearly, teachers with fewer children in their care are far more likely to provide the one-on-one attention that young children need for optimal development.

The **California** study also focused on another important determinant of program quality: provider training. Confirming similar results from other studies, researchers found that teachers with higher levels of training provided more appropriate care to young children.[12] In the 1994 report Starting Points, the Carnegie Task Force on Meeting the Needs of Young Children summarized the research on teacher education this way: "Training makes a measurable difference: when providers have learned more about how children grow and develop, they are more likely to offer warmer and more sensitive care than providers with less training."[13]

Perhaps the most important determinant of program quality, according to The National Child Care Staffing Study, involves teacher compensation. In the study, higher wages predicted better quality care. These findings are particularly relevant to state public policy development because early care providers are notoriously underpaid, despite the fact that they have higher educational levels than the U.S. workforce in general. Consequently, staff turnover rates are high. One-third of all child care teachers leave their centers each year.[14] Since young children need stable relationships with caring adults, the issues of low wages and high staff turnover are particularly important. Furthermore, the fiscal implications of adequate teacher compensation for state policy development are significant.

Although it is beyond the scope of this book to inventory all that is known to date about program quality, policymakers should be familiar with the major findings relating to program effectiveness in the long-term research. In summary, the program characteristics associated with effectiveness include:

- a program curriculum geared to the needs of young children;
- attentive and nurturing care;
- well-prepared and adequately paid staff;
- parental involvement; and
- relatively small group size.

It is important to note that the standards issued by the National Association for the Education of Young Children for program accreditation reflect the relevant research findings on quality as well as "best practice" input from professionals in the field of early care and education.[15] These standards may be useful to policymakers interested in learning more about assuring quality early care and education programs.

This publication emphasizes both the outcome and quality research because each is crucial to the implementation of effective state early care and education programs. Again, without consideration of quality factors in developing state programs, policymakers cannot be assured of achieving the public sector cost benefits cited in the outcome literature. This quality/outcome relationship will be a recurring theme throughout this book as the cross-jurisdictional implications of early care and education are addressed. Although quality programs cost money, policymakers also will pay a high price for poor quality in terms of lost benefits for individual children as well as for society at large.

Conclusion

State legislatures have assumed a pivotal leadership role in recognizing the implications of quality early childhood programs across a broad cross-section of policy areas affecting state economic development, education, crime prevention, welfare reform, public health and other social goals. Legislators are involved in every aspect of policy and programming on child care and early childhood education. State legislatures establish programs, determine target populations for services, review agency budgets, set appropriation levels and performance standards, provide regulatory and program guidelines and, more recently, advocate for coordination of child care and early childhood policies and programs as part of broader reform initiatives to support the nation's families.

CHAPTER 2

ECONOMIC AND LABOR IMPLICATIONS OF EARLY CHILDHOOD CARE AND EDUCATION

Introduction

Quality early childhood care and education programs have both short-term and long-term economic implications for states. In the short run, such services meet the needs of the work force in which increasing numbers of mothers and fathers require reliable, affordable and quality care. For the long term, research indicates that quality early care contributes to children's lifelong success, including the ability to learn, develop social skills and obtain employment; thus, these programs are also critical to long-term business interests by preparing children to enter the workplace of the future.

To maximize benefits of public expenditures on early care and education programs, state policy must address both of these functions. In other words, if state policies focus solely on increasing the child care supply for the current work force by expanding less expensive—but mediocre—services, long-range gains for a better-prepared work force will not be achieved. Long-term implications focus policy attention on the benefits of assuring quality care for young children, while simulta-neously meeting parents' needs for affordable care. Ultimately, poor quality care is unlikely to achieve either short- or long-term policy goals.

This chapter documents the rationale for a state legislative agenda on early childhood from the eco-nomic development perspective. It cites the research base for policy developments and highlights exem-plary state legislative initiatives linking early childhood policies with robust economic development and business and work force productivity.

The Economic Effects of Early Childhood Care and Education

As an industry, early childhood care and education programs generate billions of dollars within the economy by providing jobs and increasing the purchase of goods and services in the nation's communities. Among key factors to consider in examining the economic implications of early care and education are supply and demand for services, their cost, and characteristics of the early childhood work force.

"Society has a clear interest in helping ensure that more families have access to affordable, good-quality child care that not only helps parents work, but provides the developmental and educational foundation young children need."

—Robert Campbell, Vice Chairman, Johnson and Johnson
Member, Committee for Economic Development

Demand for early childhood care and education programs has increased dramatically over the past 20 years. In 1994, mothers with preschool children made up the fastest growing segment of the labor force, and among working women, 80 percent are of childbearing age.[1] Married working mothers of children under age six have increased from 36.7 percent in 1975 to 63.5 percent in 1995.[2] This growing number of working mothers is reflected in increased spending on child care. In 1993, $25.4 billion was spent on child care for children up to age 15 whose mothers worked.[3]

> "Child care teaching staff in 1992, as in 1988, continue to earn less than half as much as comparably educated women and less than one-third as much as comparably educated men in the civilian labor force."
>
> —National Center for the Early Childhood Work Force
> *The National Child Care Staffing Study Revisited*

These numbers become more meaningful when examined in terms of the cost to American families. In 1993, poor families spent up to 18 percent of their income on child care services, and higher income families paid only 7 percent.[4] Costs for one child range from $40 to $200 per family per week, or an annual average of $2,565 for family child care and $3,173 for center-based care.[5] As stated in a recent Carnegie report, "When they realize how much child care costs, most parents are astonished."[6]

In response to the demand for child care, the number of child care workers has also increased. Between 1970 and 1996, the number of child care workers increased from 395,000 to 1,194,000.[7] Despite the three-fold increase in the last two decades, the latter figure is an underestimate because it does not include unregulated family day care providers, estimated at more than 500,000 people.[8] Officials at the National Center for the Early Childhood Workforce estimate that the number of child care workers in the United States today may realistically approach three million.[9]

An overwhelming percentage of early care providers—94 percent—are women.[10] Although real wages for the highest paid child care teacher rose by 8 percent, or 66 cents/hour, between 1988 and 1992, the average annual salary for this position was $15,488, less than the official federal poverty rate of $16,592 for a family of five in 1992.[11]

From 1988 to 1994, on average, teachers gained slightly less than a 1 percent increase in wages, from $7.15 to $7.22 per hour. Real wages for teaching assistants, the fastest growing segment of the child care work force, actually declined during this period from $5.86 per hour to $5.70.[12]

Many family day care providers earn even less. Furthermore, barely a quarter of child care centers provided full health coverage for their teaching staff in 1992.[13]

Largely due to the low pay and lack of benefits, turnover averages 26 percent in the child care field, almost three times that reported by all U.S. companies (9.6 percent) and well above the rate reported for public school teachers (5.6 percent).[14]

Turnover in the early childhood field has serious implications for the quality of care experienced by young children, who need consistency in caregiving to nurture their optimum development. High worker turnover contributes to staffing shortages and an inadequate supply of certain services. Supply shortages are most acute for infants and sick children. Moreover, many experts agree that there is an overall shortage of high-quality programs, particularly for low-income children whose families have fewer resources to allocate for market costs of high-quality programs. This is especially detrimental because low-income children need such programs the most and the cost-benefit return to society from their participation is also the greatest.

Despite the real problems of low worker pay and inadequate supply of certain services, it is evident that early care and education constitutes an important and growing segment of the American economy. The question of how the early childhood industry can best function in the larger economy is the subject of some debate. Some argue that free market principles should govern the child care industry, but an increasing number of economists recognize that child care is in important respects a public good. As such, child care services share characteristics of other public goods like defense, education and police protection. Few believe that we can rely on the free market to efficiently produce public goods. For a variety of reasons—including costs and shared benefits—public goods will not be produced in adequate supply solely by the market system.

Regardless of one's beliefs about economic theory, child care currently functions with a mix of public and private providers, resources and mechanisms that provide a diverse array of services. For state lawmakers, the most pressing question is largely how to build on that infrastructure using both public and private means to improve future prospects both for the work force and for individual children while meeting the needs of working parents today.

Preparing the Future Workforce

The private sector is increasingly concerned about the failure of American education systems to prepare future employees and provide them with the skills necessary to succeed at work. Companies also are concerned about employees' work ethic and social behavior. At the same time, business is more aware that the work force is changing. The new face of business includes more women, recent immigrants and minorities. As a result, more business interests are considering the relationship between early childhood experiences and work force quality. And for good reason.

Research indicates that quality early care programs have a high payoff for business and society. According to a federal report on Head Start, "The bulk of the research shows that children who participate in early childhood education programs exhibit greater motivation toward learning and achievement and higher regard for themselves than similar children who do not."[15] Long-term research suggests that the benefits of early childhood education extend through late adolescence and young adulthood.

Again, based on comparisons of low-income children with and without early childhood education experience, those who had attended such programs were less likely to receive public assistance and were more likely to be employed or in postsecondary education programs at age 19.[16] Over the long term, children with early childhood experience hold higher vocational aspirations and demonstrate greater achievement motivation.[17] The most recent research on the High/Scope

Perry Preschool Project showed that children in the program had higher monthly earnings at age 27 than the children who did not participate in the preschool program.[18]

Such outcomes, coupled with a changing economic environment, are sparking considerable interest across the states in expanding quality early childhood care and education programs as an economic development strategy. Leading economic experts indicate that economic growth over the past two decades has been largely the result of an influx of people entering the work force, a trend that is not expected to continue. With fewer people entering the work force, each worker's productivity is increasingly critical to achieving and maintaining a competitive edge.[19]

A HIGH-QUALITY PRESCHOOL PROGRAM PAYS OFF

The most frequently cited study of both short-term and long-term benefits of early childhood education is the High/Scope Perry Preschool Study. This study followed 123 children living in poverty and at high risk of failing in school. At the beginning of the program, youngsters were randomly divided into a program group, who received a high-quality active learning preschool program, and a no-program group, who received no preschool services. Researchers then assessed the status of the two groups annually from ages three to 11, at ages 14-15, at age 19, and, most recently, at age 27, on a range of variables.

The most recent assessment, titled *Significant Benefits*, concludes that adults born in poverty who attended a high-quality, active learning preschool program at ages three and four have fewer criminal arrests, higher earnings and property wealth, and greater commitment to marriage. Over participants' lifetimes, an estimated $7.16 is saved for every dollar invested. Educational achievements were significantly different between the two groups with 71 percent vs. 54 percent completing 12th grade or higher. The key to these benefits was the quality of the program.

Furthermore, in order to compete in a more global economy, the American work force must be properly trained and educated. There is growing consensus in the states that improving workers' education and skills is the single most important objective for improving international competitiveness. Moreover, many experts indicate that it is not simply what we learn but how we learn that will help prepare the work force of the future. In both cases, the education and skills development of workers require more than remedial education and on-the-job training. Education must start earlier, with programs for young children.

Early childhood services have been shown to improve prospects for successful employment by providing critical learning and skills development capacity to children early in their lives. This is particularly important for the growing number of children living in poverty. Although these children's successful participation will be critical to the future work force, many of them are currently doomed to failure in school even before they enter kindergarten.

A decade ago, the Committee for Economic Development (CED), an independent research and educational organization made up of more than 200 major business executives and educators, issued an alarming report about prospects for the next generation of workers. The committee documented the shocking numbers of children living in poverty and the struggle school systems face in educating disadvantaged children. These business leaders were concerned that poor children would grow up to form an underclass unable to perform in the increasingly information-based and technological workplace. The report, *Children in Need*, called for an emphasis on early care and education programs, as well as increased business involvement in the public schools.[20]

More recently, other business and economic development interests have echoed CED's concerns about the quality of the future work force, calling for proactive policies. Although in the past completion of college—and even high school—were less important to performance in a largely manufacturing-based economy, the capacity of the future work force to learn and develop new skills is critical to America's standing in a more globally competitive and technology-based economy. Simply put, a solid education, critical-thinking abilities and broad skills will be required for more workers in the future, both for their successful careers and for a thriving American economy. With fewer people entering the labor force—as demographics indicate—each worker's productivity becomes more critical. Thus, unless business taps the academic potential of additional disadvantaged children, critical labor shortages will stymie economic performance.

Providing quality early care experiences for young

SKILLS FOR THE FUTURE

In the future, workers need to "possess a solid basic education, broad skills, flexibility and be cross-trained in different areas," says Brian Bosworth, former president of the Indiana Economic Development Council.[21] Countries successful in global economic markets accomplish this by linking education with economic development strategy. Bosworth explains that in countries like Japan, where companies value an "individual's ability to learn, the academic system emphasizes fundamentals, theoretical analysis, and the techniques of learning."[22]

children is an important option for improving academic and vocational performance and, as such, is a critical element in a broad-based strategy to link education, economic development and work force preparation.

To address concerns about education and preparation of the work force, the U.S. Secretary of Labor's Commission on Achieving Necessary Skills issued a 1991 report emphasizing a contemporary approach to learning in public schools. This approach identifies three principles to guide contextual learning:

1. Students need to learn basic skills and problem-solving concurrently;

2. Learning should be directed toward problem-solving, not just mastering simple information; and

3. Students need practice in applying skills they are learning.[23]

These principles are surprisingly similar to effective early childhood education curriculum, such as that used in the High/Scope Perry Preschool Project. The High/Scope curriculum emphasizes active learning within a "plan-do-review" approach. The focus is not only on what children learn but how they learn and on developing capacities to apply learning to multiple subject areas.

"What we know and can do holds the key to economic progress, just as command of natural resources once did," explain Ray Marshall and Marc Tucker.[24] How people learn, what they learn and where they learn are important not only in school but on the job and in their personal lives. Throughout life, it is the ability to solve problems and apply information to other areas that defines both career and personal success. As Marshall and Tucker say, "The future now belongs to societies that organize themselves for learning,"[25] and early childhood care and education are the first step.

State Legislative Initiatives in Work Force Preparation

A growing number of state legislatures have responded to early childhood program research by linking service expansion with broader economic development initiatives. This section highlights legislative actions in two neighboring states: **Oregon** and **Washington.** In **Oregon,** early childhood policy was integrated with a larger, comprehensive economic development package, while **Washington**'s initiative focused more narrowly on linking economic development with early care and education. Either state strategy can be effective in strengthening state policy on early care and education. The **Oregon** legislature enacted a unique system of outcome measures—called benchmarks—to guide the direction of state government into the 21st century. Within this large-scale, results-oriented strategy, high priority is given to early childhood education. In **Washington**, a comprehensive preschool program for at-risk four-year-olds was created primarily as a specific economic development strategy.

Oregon

To achieve a productive and competitive work force, argues R. Scott Foster of the Committee for Economic Development, requires a comprehensive blueprint for human investment throughout the life cycle, from early childhood throughout adolescence into adulthood. To meet this challenge, Foster suggests a three-pronged approach: (1) invest in children, youth and families; (2) promote productivity in the current work force through the provision of child care; and (3) assist older workers in remaining active and productive.

Oregon's 1991 legislative action reflects Foster's lifelong approach. The legislature adopted the benchmarks, a strategic plan for economic development with a goal of "developing the best work force in the U.S. by the year 2000 and equal to any in the world by 2010."[26] Furthermore, the **Oregon** benchmarks are groundbreaking because they represent a comprehensive attempt by the legislature to set budget and public policy priorities systematically based on measurable outcomes that recognize interrelationships among education, economic development, early childhood development and other state policy areas.

The goal of the benchmarks is to encourage state and local budgeting to focus on programs with a high payoff in terms of:

- their contribution to an individual's self-sufficiency, knowledge, and quality of life;
- contribution to local and state economies; and
- reductions in future program costs (prevention).[27]

Benchmarks cover policies in all areas of state government. Of the numerous benchmarks originally enacted, some are identified as "urgent," or high priority for the legislature. One of these urgent benchmarks is early childhood education.

New policy on early childhood education, known as the Early Childhood Improvement Program, is included in the 1991 Oregon Educational Act for the 21st Century. In order to assure quality programs, the legislation specifically requires that programs "be based on research and proven successful practices in programs such as Head Start." Programs must also be evaluated for effectiveness. Other mandated program components include (1) targeting services for "at-risk" children; (2) improving curriculum and educational practices in kindergarten through third grade to reflect research about how children learn and to exhibit sensitivity to cultural differences, different learning styles and individual differences; and (3) encouraging parental participation.[28]

In addition, the legislature established phased implementation. Half of all children eligible for state prekindergarten programs must be enrolled in either state prekindergarten or Head Start by 1999, and all eligible children must be served by 2004.[29] Consistent with Head Start standards, **Oregon**'s Pre-K program provides comprehensive education, social and health services to low-income three- and four-year-old children. Total funding for **Oregon** prekindergarten is currently around $52.7 million for the 1995-97 biennium. This appropriation for prekindergarten amounts to slightly more than one-third of total public spending on early childhood education in the state, with federal funds for Head Start making up the remaining two-thirds.[30]

Movement toward universal coverage in prekindergarten has been stymied by **Oregon**'s Ballot Measure 5, which curtails property tax assessments. As a result of the ballot measure, flexibility to appropriate funds for new or expanding programs has been limited.[31] At the same time, statutory requirements to establish and maintain quality in early childhood programming demand certain fiscal resources. Within the context of such fiscal constraints, recent appropriations have focused on maintaining program quality rather than expanding the program. As a result, only 29 percent of eligible children are being served with state prekindergarten or Head Start in 1996-97.[32] Still, the **Oregon** example illustrates that setting benchmarks for early childhood education allows a state to measure progress in this important area.

Washington

The **Washington** Early Childhood Education and Assistance Program (ECEAP) provides low-income four-year-old children with a comprehensive preschool experience to prepare them to succeed in school. The initiative was conceived in 1986, propelled by concern for the quality of the future work force in a depressed economy plagued by high unemployment and a recession.

PRESCHOOL IMPROVES LEARNING ABILITIES

Children who had participated in **Washington**'s Early Childhood Education and Assistance Program, a comprehensive preschool program for low-income four-year-olds, had significantly higher scores in language and motor skills and conceptual abilities than children who had not attended a comprehensive preschool and who came from more advantaged homes.

The Washington Roundtable, a nonprofit research and policy development organization of corporate executives, provided the impetus for a movement "to examine the state's economic outlook and to evaluate the education system's ability to supply future workers with the skills needed in a more diversified, complex, and competitive economic environment."[33] The state's business leaders were convinced by longitudinal studies, such as the High/Scope Perry Preschool evaluation that suggests that quality early childhood experiences for at-risk preschoolers can result in long-term savings and improved outcomes. The roundtable's top legislative priority was a state-funded preschool program for at-risk four-year-olds modeled on Head Start.

The bill received bipartisan support. The success of its adoption is attributed to advocacy by legislators, the Washington Roundtable, the governor and active lobbying by a coalition of education reform advocates, Head Start providers and citizen and community groups.[34]

To reinforce the relationship between the early

childhood initiative and economic development goals, the program was placed in the Department of Community, Trade and Economic Development. To work toward quality programming, ECEAP adheres to standards issued by the National Association for the Education of Young Children (NAEYC).[35] Emphasis on program outcomes is reflected in a statutory requirement to evaluate programs rigorously by comparing outcomes for participants with those of children who do not participate. The most recent evaluation of the program revealed these highlights:

Children's language skills, conceptual abilities, motor skills and receptive vocabulary improved dramatically during their ECEAP year. In three areas—language, concepts and motor skills—the childrens' development surpassed the national average for their age group.

At the start of kindergarten, ECEAP children had significantly higher scores in these areas than peers who had not participated in a comprehensive preschool program and who came from significantly more advantaged homes.[36]

As evaluations document program effectiveness, state appropriations for the program continue to increase. In 1985, when the legislation was enacted, $38,000 was appropriated for planning.[37] Since then, state funding has increased from $2.97 million in FY 1986-87 to $28.3 million in FY 1996-97, and the number of children served has grown from 1,000 to 7,032.[38] Like Head Start, children are eligible for ECEAP if their family's income is below the federal poverty level.

With ECEAP and Head Start funds combined, **Washington** is providing early childhood education to nearly all eligible four-year-olds in the state as estimated by U.S. Census data. However, the exact percentage is difficult to estimate because state administrators believe that the census seriously undercounted eligible children. This is reflected by waiting lists in every region and by locally conducted needs assessments.[39] Even so, ECEAP and Head Start in **Washington** serve a substantial majority of four-year-olds under the federal poverty level, somewhere between 60 percent and 85 percent. Program representatives suggest that a major reason for increased appropriations has been the documentation of positive program outcomes in regular evaluations required by the legislation.[40]

Child Care and the Current Work Force

Child care is also a factor in improving workers' productivity. To be employed parents need affordable child care. A variety of studies suggest that child care helps companies recruit and retain workers, improves workers' productivity, reduces absenteeism and tardiness and can actually save money for companies that provide assistance. Consider the following:

- A 1996 General Accounting Office (GAO) report indicated that a lack of adequate child care affects clients' ability to complete job training successfully.[41] In a separate 1994 study, the GAO also found that child care subsidies are crucial for successful welfare reform.[42] GAO predicted that a full child care subsidy increases by 15-percentage points in the average probability of poor mothers' working.[43]

- A 1991 Department of Labor survey found that for approximately one-quarter of unemployed mothers in their 20s child care problems tended to keep them out of work longer than other problems.[44]

- A 1992 survey found that nearly 30 percent of workers knew employees who quit their jobs because of inadequate child care. The same survey indicated that high percentages of workers also experienced lower productivity and higher absenteeism and tardiness because of child care problems.[45]

- Child care issues are cited by employers as causing more problems than any other family-related issue in the work-place, with increases in absenteeism and tardiness reported in nine out of 10 companies. Eighty percent of the companies surveyed said that work days were cut short because of child care problems.[46]

- A 1994 report identified child care as the top concern of workers when transferred by their employer.[47]

- A 1992 GAO report found that songle parents who received child care assistance, either through the federal Job Training Partnership Act (JTPA) or elsewhere, more often successfully completed their training, obtained jobs or experienced other positive outcomes, such as returning school.[48]

More and more businesses are responding to these issues by addressing attention to their employees' child care needs. In the first controlled cost-benefit study ever conducted on a corporate on-site child care center, the Union Bank in Pasadena, Calif., saved between $138,000 and $232,000 annually in operations, attributed mostly to reduced turnover and absenteeism.[49] Another **California** company reported $11,000 in savings in 1992 from an on-site child care center because of reduced turnover and tax credits.[50]

Since demographic trends indicate that women have become an important segment of the work force and are expected to stay there, a growing number of businesses are exploring ways to support family child care needs. These options range from on-site care to flexible benefits for child care expenses.

According to a recent study, the number of companies offering child care options for employers nearly tripled in a recent four-year period. Approximately 30 percent of firms said they offered child care assistance in 1992, compared with around 10 percent in 1988, partly to enhance productivity.[51]

Recent evidence indicates that a number of U.S. companies are focusing on quality in developing child care services for their employees. For example, a 1993

> "When a company establishes a child care center for its employees, it wants high quality and that requires an investment of time and money,"
>
> —Marcia Brumit Knopf, Research Director
> Catalyst, a New York City-based research group

study of 91 firms indicates that private sector sponsorship of child care programs often improves program quality by focusing on staff/child ratios, group sizes and staff training.[52]

Today, more than 80 companies, including some of the nation's largest, are involved in a collaborative effort to develop new child care and preschool programs. The collaboration has spent nearly $25 million supporting quality by supporting the National Association for the Education of Young Children (NAEYC) accreditation standards for teacher training.[53]

Many states have launched early childhood initiatives that focus on expanding the availability of child care for the current work force. In expanding child care options for workers, lawmakers most frequently focus on:

- public/private initiatives that provide incentives for providers or for employer-supported assistance; and

• expanding child care supply for low-income workers.

The former strategy is designed to leverage private support for certain employees, while the latter focuses public sector activity on a targeted group with few resources to pay market costs of child care. Both options attempt to increase the overall supply of child care for working parents.

Selected Legislative Public/Private Child Care Initiatives

State lawmakers can provide incentives and direction to providers and employers to provide child care assistance and to make the work environment responsive to family needs. The following illustrates state approaches to provide incentives to the private sector.

Loan Programs

At least 11 states have implemented loan programs in order to increase the supply of child care services in the private sector. **Maryland**'s Day Care Loan Guarantee Fund is available to corporations, businesses and individual proprietors to develop or expand child care facilities.[54] Since 1985, 57 loans have been guaranteed through the program, creating 3,729 spaces.[55] In one case, a facility created by 10 area employers used the fund both for start-up and later expansion.[56] The guarantee program was so successful that the state created a direct loan program as well; that program has financed 34 loans serving 4,084 children since 1989.[57] Currently the appropriation for the direct loan program is $650,000 for FY 1997.[58] **Arkansas, California, Connecticut, Florida, Maine, Maryland, New Hampshire, New York, North Carolina, Tennessee,** and **Washington** have loan programs.[59]

Grant Programs

States also use grant programs to expand the availability of services. **Rhode Island**'s Human Services Department administers a grant program for development of licensed child care facilities in industrial parks.[60] **Florida** created a matching grant program for private employers who contribute to an employee's child care costs. It allows employers to apply for a grant of up to 50 percent of the amount paid, with a ceiling of $100,000 per employer.[61] In 1990, the state allocated one-third of the funds to small businesses.[62]

New Jersey's small grant program, the Mini Child Care Centers (MCCC), provides technical assistance and cash grants to applicants who want to either start a mini child care center (10-35 children) or increase the licensed capacity of one. The program has created 481 new child care slots increasing licensed capacity from an average of 11.1 slots per program to an average of 29.6 licensed slots per program.[63]

Corporate Tax Incentives

Eighteen states have implemented corporate tax credits or deductions in an attempt to encourage employers to expand child care options for their employees. **Florida** corporations may deduct 100 percent of the start-up costs of an on-site child care facility.[64] **Oregon** created a 50 percent tax credit for corporations that provide or pay for child care services for their employees. Under the plan, employees may choose any licensed provider. After paying for the services, corporations are allowed a credit up to $1,250 per full-time employee.[65] **Arkansas** enacted several tax incentives for businesses that create or operate on-site child care facilities in 1993. Companies with on-site facilities may receive a corporate tax credit of 3.9 percent of the salaries of employees who work at the facility and exemptions from sales and use taxes for building construction and furnishings.[66] At least 14 other states have enacted employer tax credits.

One problem faced by states implementing such tax credit policies is poor utilization.[67] A study by the Child Care Action Campaign found that employer tax credits have had only a marginal impact on the supply of child care. Credits are underutilized by businesses because of their administrative costs, and their focus on start-up rather than ongoing operational expenses. Also, credits only affect businesses with corporate tax liability, which eliminates many employers. For example, in **Michigan** less than half of employers are actually liable for corporate taxes.[68]

Space Allocation Policies

Space allocation policies require or encourage certain developers to set space aside for child care centers in business sites. As a model for other employers, **California** and **Maryland** require an allocation of space in new state buildings for child care use. **Massachusetts** allows the child care portion of a development to be taxed at the residential rate rather than the commercial rate imposed on the rest of the building.[69]

Personnel Policies

An increasing number of lawmakers are exploring personnel policies to prompt employers to help meet the child care needs of their employees. For example, **Washington** requires certain employers to allow employees to use sick leave to care for children who are ill.[70]

State Employees

A few states have passed laws to establish on-site or near-site child care for state employees, usually at state agency buildings or universities. Such legislation has been approved in **California, Oklahoma, Texas** and **Washington**.[71] Employers have the option of offering federal income reduction plans to their employees. Under such a plan, funds earmarked for child care expenses are withheld from the employee's gross income. Neither payroll nor personal income taxes are paid on the funds withheld, thereby reducing the cost of care to the employee. Some states allow state employees to use the federal plan.

Information Referral and Technical Assistance

Lack of information is a major barrier to increasing private sector involvement in child care: corporations and other employers may not understand the relationship of quality early childhood care and education to worker productivity.

Legislation to create state information clearinghouses is growing.

- **Texas** authorizes the employment commission to provide technical assistance to employers regarding child care employee benefits.

- **Arkansas** launched a public awareness program directed at child care services for special needs children.

- **Washington** has created an office of child care resources within the Department of Social and Health Services, which provides materials to educate employers and parents about employer-supported child care.[72]

At least 21 state legislatures appropriate funds to support child care resource and referral agencies (R & Rs) and information and referral networks.[73] This strategy is designed to connect working parents with existing child care resources and to educate them about quality issues to help improve their role as informed consumers. R & Rs also provide training to child care providers and work in their local businesses and philanthropic communities to stimulate the supply of needed services.

Case Study: Maine Improves Low-Income Child Care

Maine's 1993 legislative initiative (1993 Me. Laws, Chap. 158) was designed to increase the supply of affordable quality child care for low-income parents. The law was shepherded through the Joint Human Services Committee with key support from the state's business community. The legislation helps low-income parents by increasing the availability of and access to publicly provided child care services. The following are some key provisions of the law:

- Expediting the process of connecting families with publicly funded child care programs by requiring the state to determine their eligibility within 30 days of their application;

- Encouraging quality by allowing higher public reimbursement rates to providers who adhere to nationally recognized quality standards;

- Funding the state's child care resource and referral agencies to help connect parents with quality providers; and

- Prohibiting the use of federal funds to replace existing state funds, thereby assuring that more child care services will be available.

STRATEGIES FOR DEVELOPING CHILD CARE POLICIES

Enacting legislation on early care issues is not always easy. **Maine's** two-year effort to adopt new policy on comprehensive child care services involved four important strategies:

- Developing consensus among state advocacy groups;

- Educating a broad cadre of legislators with a concerted effort to involve leadership and the chairs of relevant committees;

- Garnering support and involvement of key state business leaders; and

- Developing an interjurisdictional team of legislators, legislative staff, agencies and advocates.

Before the legislation was passed, there was a power struggle between the legislative and executive branch over use of federal funds and the provision of child care services to low-income families. To balance the decision making process, the new statute requires ongoing legislative participation in a state advisory committee that reviews and plans for federal child care funds. This involvement is crucial to maintaining a legislative perspective in policy and program administration.

Motivated by the need to provide dependable and affordable child care for working families, former Representative Edward Pineau, a member of the Joint Committee on Labor, spearheaded the effort to enact this bill. He formed an ad hoc committee of state advocates, providers, legislators and agency representatives and held two statewide public hearings to get broad input in identifying the most pressing issues in early care and education. Building consensus within the early childhood community is not easy, but it is essential in developing effective policy that can be supported by affected stakeholders. According to Pineau, "Bringing advocates together with a singular voice was probably the most important strategy for passage of comprehensive child care legislation."[74]

With funds from the Carnegie Corporation and the Foundation for Child Development, Representative Pineau attracted experts from the National Conference of State Legislatures (NCSL) and the Children's Defense Fund (CDF) to analyze **Maine**'s system and build consensus among stakeholders in the child care community. Representative Pineau arranged a well-attended workshop for legislators, advocates, child care providers, agency personnel and parents where staff from CDF and NCSL provided both a national perspective and substantive information on technical, but critical, child care issues.

Legislative authority was critical to the adoption of new child care policies in **Maine**, since the executive branch was providing little leadership. Particularly at issue in the state was planning for the use of new federal child care funds available for low-income and welfare families. Some child care advocates were concerned that new federal dollars were not being earmarked to expand state child care services and that the executive branch was not seeking input from all the stakeholders. In examining state policy, key legislative support included the senate majority leader and chairs of the Education and Labor Committees in both chambers.

In contrast to solid legislative support, the governor was resistant to the bill's adoption. To counter this opposition, bill sponsors involved business leaders in garnering support. The Maine Bankers Association was recruited to sponsor a meeting of business leaders and legislators on child care. The keynote speaker was the influential Arnold Hiatt, chairman of the Stride Rite Foundation and pioneer of employer-supported child care. His address emphasized the importance of child care not only to workers, but to business and the economy. Strong state business support was critical to the adoption of the child care reform package in **Maine**.

Conclusion

Early care and education make up an important and growing segment of the American economy. Ideally, state legislative policies on early care and education perform a dual function of preparing children to be the future work force, while supporting their parents as the current workers. Future policy issues are likely to include growing service demands, job growth in the industry, costs of quality and worker compensation. The Bureau of Labor Statistics projects that the number of child care workers will increase by 65.8 percent from 1994 to 2005, which is three times the rate of overall projected job growth.[75] As the industry mushrooms, issues related to assuring quality service to meet dual policy purposes will continue to demand significant state legislative leadership and innovation. Lawmakers must balance policies to assist working parents now, while preparing their children for the workplaces of tomorrow.

CHAPTER 3

THE IMPLICATIONS OF EARLY CHILDHOOD SERVICES AND SCHOOL-AGE CHILD CARE FOR PUBLIC EDUCATION

Introduction

For current and future generations of young people, the ability to think creatively, adapt learning and perform academically has become more crucial than it ever was for their parents. For both the individual and American society, future success is predicated on the capacity to function in an increasingly competitive and technology-based global economy. America can no longer afford the proportion of high school dropouts who leave the public school system annually nor the number of graduates who enter the work force without basic and adaptable skills.

With education expenditures accounting for 42.6 percent of state budgets, state legislators are increasingly concerned about poor academic outcomes and their impact on future prosperity, and they are demanding more from state education systems. Over the past two decades, state lawmakers have led the movement to reform and restructure public education in an effort to increase its effectiveness and efficiency.

At the same time, increasing research evidence suggests that the foundation for academic success is laid well before a child enters the public schools. A recent report from the Carnegie Corporation of New York outlines the research base on the value of early education and concludes that a child's early years are crucial to brain development and, as a consequence, to prepare the child for formal learning and academic achievement.[1] Within this context, increas-

ing state policy attention is being given to quality early childhood education services—programs that have repeatedly been shown to increase children's prospects for future school accomplishments.

State lawmakers are also experimenting with new ways of using the public education infrastructure to meet family and social needs through expanding options for child care for school-age children and school-linked or -based social services for children and their families. Though school-age child care programs are increasingly in demand by two-worker families, the best programs are

> Education systems are being called on more often to address complex social problems that previously did not exist or were handled in other settings.

also intended to meet students' needs for stimulating developmental experiences that will benefit them in other areas, including academics and social adjustment.

WHAT IS SCHOOL READINESS?

Many factors contribute to a child's success in school. A task force of the National Association of State Boards of Education defines school readiness as far more than academic knowledge and skills. Readiness is based on children's physical health, self-confidence and social competence. It is not determined solely by the innate abilities and capacities of young children. Readiness is shaped and developed by people and environments in the early childhood years. Self-confidence, the ability to make plans and anticipate consequences and the ability to cooperate with staff and peers are the key factors in early childhood success.

—National Association of State Boards of Education
Caring Communities: Supporting Young Children and Families

School-linked or school-based social service programs have a broad purpose: to enhance students' ability to learn by improving their access to adequate health care, appropriate recreation and a nurturing family life. By meeting such needs it is expected that students—and sometimes parents—will be more capable of learning. School-linked programs frequently offer classes to assist parents in their nurturing and teaching roles; health services, screening, or referral; student tutoring or mentoring; and specialized programs—like parental literacy or English proficiency classes—for specific populations. Some programs offer child care for the children of teenage students to increase graduation rates for this at-risk population.

The overriding goal of both school-linked family service programs and school-age child care services is to find new, more effective methods of improving academic outcomes to prevent future social problems and their associated costs. To date, however, there is little research evidence regarding program outcomes, largely because school-age child care and school-linked family services are relatively new programs. At the heart of the debate, however, is consideration of the public school system as a logical and efficient place to link services that help prepare young children to start school, enrich a child's public school education and provide services to help children stay in school.

This chapter explores the movement to link public education with the following areas:

- Early childhood services, especially state-funded preschool programs and state funding for Head Start;
  - Before- and after-school care for school-age children; and
  - Early child care services for the children of teen parents as one example of the developing movement toward broad-based school-linked social services.

The rationale and research basis for linkage is discussed and state examples are provided throughout the chapter to illustrate trends in state policymaking to address learning within the context of the whole child and family.

It should be recognized, however, that policymakers are not all in agreement about the merits of tapping the public education infrastructure for early childhood services or additional social service responsibilities. Some argue that the public education system is already overwhelmed and should concentrate on a more basic notion of education, and some suggest that other providers are better able to advocate for families and serve their social service needs than the education bureaucracy. Others, in contrast, argue that the public schools are well positioned to provide early childhood care and education. Nonetheless, in an increasing number of states, legislators are exercising their role as state policy innovators to link early childhood, social services and child care with public education systems. Some of the most promising options offer new ways for the existing education, social service and child caring systems to collaborate on behalf of children and families.

Early Childhood Education: A Stepping-Stone to School Success

Public concern about children and youth failing in school is at an all-time high. The National Dropout Prevention Center estimates that 25 percent of students drop out of high school.[2] Students from low-income families are 2.4 times more likely to drop out of school than are children from middle-income families, and 10.5 times more likely than students from high-income families. For high-risk populations, dropout rates are even higher, such as 29.3 percent for Hispanics.[3] Although the American public has traditionally supported free universal education for children from kindergarten through grade 12, the public perception is that the nation's public schools are in trouble. Furthermore, educators claim that it is becoming more and more difficult for schools to succeed with increasing numbers of ill-prepared or troubled children coming to school.

In a survey conducted by the Carnegie Foundation for the Advancement of Teaching, kindergarten teachers reported a dramatic increase in the numbers of children unprepared for the school environment. In the survey results, 43 percent of teachers said that their students are not as well prepared for school as their earlier counterparts.[4] Both children and the educational institutions are thus at a disadvantage for achieving success.

State policymakers are recognizing that what happens to children in their early years has a significant effect not just on the children themselves but also on the education system. From a public policy standpoint, this is particularly important for children who are most at risk of school failure— children from low-income families, children whose parents never completed high school, children who face discrimination because of their color and children from dysfunctional families.

higher on intelligence tests through the primary grades and higher on achievement tests in eighth grade.[5] In addition, economically disadvantaged children with early childhood education experience are less likely to be placed in special education classes, classified as mentally retarded and held back during elementary school.[6] This, in turn, gives children a better chance to succeed in later grades.

And over the long term, research indicates that low-income children who attend early childhood education programs score higher on achievement tests, earn higher grade-point averages and are more likely to complete high school.[7] Moreover, children in many studies show greater initiative and assertiveness and feel better about themselves than those who have not attended early childhood education programs.[8]

Although the most significant factor influencing state political support for early childhood education has

---

EDUCATIONAL RESULTS: HIGH/SCOPE PERRY PRESCHOOL STUDY

By age 27	Program	Nonprogram
Years of schooling	11.9	11.0
On-time high school graduation	66%	45%
High school graduation or GED	71%	54%
Postsecondary credits	33%	28%

Students who participated in the preschool project—especially females—stayed in school longer and had a higher rate of graduation from high school than those who didn't participate.

—Lawrence J. Schweinhart et al., *Significant Benefits*

Research Findings

To date, most research on early childhood programs has focused on high-risk populations that are more likely to fail academically and in other areas. Research from major longitudinal studies on the impact of quality early childhood programs on high-risk populations confirms a remarkable ameliorative effect, particularly with respect to enhancing children's ability to succeed in school.

In the most prominent study, conducted by the High/Scope Educational Research Foundation in Ypsilanti, Mich., low-income, African-American children who participated in quality early childhood education programs in the High/Scope Perry Preschool Project scored

been the research demonstrating short- and long-term academic and social benefits to disadvantaged three- and four-year-olds, the projected cost-savings are equally significant. Based on the High/Scope Perry Preschool Project and other research, the Committee on Economic Development reported in 1991 that "for every $1 spent on a comprehensive and intensive preschool program for the disadvantaged, society saves up to $6 in the long-term costs of welfare, remedial education, teen pregnancy, and crime."[9] In 1993, the most recent High/Scope Perry Preschool research estimated that the program saved $6,872 per participant in elementary and secondary education costs alone.[10] Savings include lower costs of special education and remedial services and reductions in the number of students repeating grades.

Armed with such research findings, state legislatures have taken the initiative to create and fund state preschool programs or to supplement federal Head Start programs with state money. According to the Children's Defense Fund, 25 states and the **District of Columbia** have funded state preschool programs, and 13 states and the **District of Columbia** supplement Head Start programs. State funding for the 1991-92 school year amounted to $665 million, with $611 million devoted to state preschool and $54 million earmarked for Head Start supplements.[11] Both strategies expand the number of low-income children served in early education programs.

Despite its significant impact on low-income populations, both state and federal policymakers have struggled to provide early education services for an increasing number of disadvantaged children. Though public investments in services have increased significantly in recent years, the number of poor preschool-age children has increased by 28 percent.[12] Although the research suggests that providing quality preschool to low-income children results in the greatest individual and societal gains, it is precisely these poorer children who still lack access to programs. According to a 1993 report issued by the General Accounting Office about 35 percent of all poor three- and four-year-olds participated in preschool, compared with over 60 percent of the highest income three- and four-year-olds.[13]

State Legislative Initiatives: Early Education

Today, state legislatures are continuing a history of commitment to early childhood education. Long before the term school readiness was popularized by the National Education Goals established by President George Bush and the 50 governors, legislatures had created and funded preschool programs. State legislative commitment to early care and education is illustrated by the investment of nearly $700 million in public money in such programs in 1991-92.[14] State legislatures in 25 states and the **District of Columbia** appropriated funds for preschool programs, despite an environment of fiscal austerity at the time, in many of those jurisdictions. Most state statutes focus on services to at-risk populations. In addition, 13 states and the **District of Columbia** supple-

ment federally funded Head Start programs in order to increase the quality of programs or expand the number of children served.[15]

Since 1991-92 when the Children's Defense Fund surveyed the states about prekindergarten programs, additional states, including **Delaware, Georgia,** and **Virginia** have funded state prekindergarten programs. **Tennessee** legislators approved an early childhood education program for 3- and 4-year-olds, and the state will begin implementation in 1997. **North Carolina** appropriated funds for Head Start agencies to expand facilities.[16]

State actions to create early education programs reflect different political climates, demographics and geography. The states described here are intended to provide a sampling of various approaches. **Kentucky** is an example of a relatively poor, primarily rural state that has created a statewide preschool program within a larger education reform initiative. **Ohio** represents a larger, more urban jurisdiction that provides both generous supplements to Head Start programs and funding for a state preschool program. **Georgia's** approach attempts to connect public schools and child care providers through a unique financing mechanism to serve preschool to all 4-year-olds.

Kentucky

Kentucky's state-funded preschool program was enacted as part of the Kentucky Education Reform Act (KERA) of 1990, a groundbreaking education reform initiative that— among other reforms—redesigned the structure of the state's system to incorporate outcomes-based accountability. The reform legislation is particularly notable for linking improved academic performance with the provision of school readiness, health and other social services. In addition to creating the preschool program, the legislation also mandated development of family resource centers at all low-income schools (see chapter 8).

The legislature chose to create a state program, rather than simply supplement Head Start, for two reasons: (1) to maintain state control of the program (performance and accountability) and (2) to support the school-based decision making, local flexibility and autonomy initiated under the larger education reform structure.[17] School districts must, however, work with Head Start to recruit students and have the discretion to collaborate with Head Start providers in delivering services. As a result, approximately 50 percent of the

STATES THAT FUND STATE PRESCHOOLS OR SUPPLEMENT HEAD START PROGRAMS

States That Fund Preschools (26)*

Arizona	Louisiana	Oklahoma
Arkansas	Maine	Oregon
California	Maryland	Rhode Island
Colorado	Massachusetts	South Carolina
District of Columbia	Michigan	Texas
Florida	New Jersey	Vermont
Illinois	New Mexico	Washington
Iowa	New York	West Virginia
Kentucky	Ohio	

States That Supplement Head Start Programs (13 and the District of Columbia)

Alaska	Minnesota
Connecticut	New Hampshire
Florida	Ohio
Hawaii	Rhode Island
Illinois	Washington
Maine	Wisconsin
Massachusetts	

States That Do Both (8)

District of Columbia
Florida
Illinois
Maine
Massachusetts
Ohio
Rhode Island
Washington

Source: Children's Defense Fund

*Delaware, Georgia, and Virginia have funded programs since this survey was conducted. North Carolina has funded Head Start.

school districts have collaborative arrangements with Head Start providers. In about half the districts, state-funded children and federally funded Head Start children actually attend the same classes. In these blended classrooms, costs are shared between both funding sources, although separate audit trails are maintained. Program personnel report that blending reduces service duplication and costs, and results in improved classroom facilities.[18]

The legislature has been aggressive in funding the preschool program. Since its inception six years ago, funding has increased by 155 percent, from $14.5 million in state expenditures in 1990-91 to $38.1 million in 1996-97. Program eligibility is limited to four-year-olds in families whose income is below 130 percent of the federal poverty level and to three- and four-year-old children with any developmental delays, regardless of income.[19] Of the total number of children eligible, approximately 27,600 children were served by KERA and Head Start partnerships as of December 1995. This number represents 74 percent of income-eligible children and 96 percent of all preschoolers with any delays. These percentages served are remarkable, given that nearly three quarters of **Kentucky**'s four-year-olds actually meet the eligibility requirements.[20]

In order to assure statewide consistency in quality—whether a child is served directly by the school district or through another agency like Head Start—all programs must meet minimum standards. These cover such areas as comprehensive health services, nutrition, social services, parental involvement, staff qualifications and developmentally appropriate practice. Generally programs are half-day, but most transport children to child care within the school district. In one-quarter of the school districts state preschool programs work with family resource centers to offer child care for the remainder of the day. All school districts have interagency groups to coordinate child care, Head Start and preschool. The **Kentucky** preschool program requires a staff/child ratio of 1:10.[21] In blended classrooms (state-funded and Head Start children) the highest program standards apply.[22]

Initial research results, based on a three-year evaluation of the program, show positive outcomes for the children who participate in **Kentucky**'s preschool program. Achievement scores for preschool children are equal to or higher than their other classmates in kindergarten and first grade. Program children particularly excelled in expressive communication, social skills and familiarity with books—all areas related to success in school and in life.[23]

WHAT IS DEVELOPMENTALLY APPROPRIATE PRACTICE?

According to Dr. Meera Mani, director of the Clayton Charter School in Denver, Colo., developmentally appropriate activities are those suited to the age, the developmental stage and the learning style of every individual child. Too often, early childhood programs are organized solely around a child's chronological age, without consideration of the child's developmental stage or learning style. A developmental stage is a more complex concept than age, encompassing the child's current level of cognitive, emotional, social and physical functioning. Learning style refers to how children master concepts and information—some learn by listening and observing, others learn through hands-on activity. In its position statement on developmentally appropriate practice, the National Association for the Education of Young Children recommends that the curriculum emphasize interactive learning for children, where children can learn through active exploration and interaction with adults, other children and materials. Developmentally appropriate practices consider all factors—age, developmental stage, learning style and appropriate curriculum.

Ohio

The Ohio legislature has embarked on an ambitious strategy to provide early childhood programs to low-income children, using a two-fold policy strategy. The state not only appropriates significant dollars to supplement Head Start but also funds a smaller state-operated preschool program. Supplementing Head Start is a way for the state to serve more children in a program proven effective in preparing children for kindergarten. The purpose of funding a separate state preschool program is to expand eligibility to additional low-income children and to maintain variety among program operators.

Ohio's policy strategy regarding Head Start is among the most ambitious in the nation. The state has committed to serve 100 percent of Head Start-eligible children whose families want these services by 1999 with either Head Start or state preschool funds. To reach this goal, the state recently appropriated about $145 million to supplement Head Start programs over a two-year period.[24] This funding level will serve 75 percent of all children eligible for Head Start in 1996-97, far ahead of the national average of 35 percent.[25] In adopting this strategy, the legislature maintains control over state expenditures by requiring by law an annual on-site review of Head Start providers.[26]

Appropriations for the state preschool program are $33 million for fiscal years 1996 and 1997. When these preschool funds are added to the state's Head Start investment, 79 percent of Ohio's eligible children are now served.[27] In an effort to assure program comprehensiveness, including health and social services, and to promote quality, the preschool program is statutorily required to conform to Head Start standards. Unlike Kentucky, it is unusual for children in state preschool programs to attend classes with Head Start students. Even though standards are the same, those familiar with the program believe that mixing children from different programs makes fiscal management overly cumbersome.[28] It is becoming more common, however, for preschool and Head Start students to share joint activities and for programs to be located in the same building.[29]

Even with the state's significant fiscal commitment to preschool and Head Start services, Ohio (like many other states) grapples with the challenge of balancing the child care needs of low-income families with their children's needs for early education. Since Head Start is usually a half-day program, many low-income parents still lack child care during the remainder of the day. The state increased funding for child care for welfare recipients by nearly $65 million over the previous biennium and by $10 million for low-income care.[30] Yet some legislators are concerned that there may not be enough child care money to combine with half day Head Start and preschool programs in order to meet the full-day needs of working parents.[31] This issue has implications for the state and federal welfare to work policy, where parents often need child care to keep their jobs.

One way states have addressed this policy dilemma is by using public low-income child care funds or other state resources to extend Head Start program hours. This strategy is often referred to as "wraparound." Two years after a failed legislative attempt to earmark 25 percent of new Head Start funds for child care wraparound services, legislators reached agreement with the governor on a slightly different approach. The 1995 budget earmarks $6 million per year over the current biennium for full day Head Start or preschool; $3 million is dedicated from the

Head Start budget and $3 million is from the welfare to work budget.[32] Though these amounts may not completely meet low-income parents' full-day needs, **Ohio** legislators took the lead in addressing the issue. To help implement the wraparound services, the state Department of Education developed five specific models for collaboration between child care, Head Start and preschool.[33]

This need for full-day services for children illustrates that the distinction between child care and early education programs is becoming extinct. Especially in an environment of work requirements and time limits for welfare recipients, today's early care programs must focus both on education and on meeting the needs of working parents. In **Ohio** policymakers are working toward a comprehensive early care and education system. As a first step, Head Start grantees and public preschool providers will be encouraged to provide Head Start services for part of the day and child care for the remainder of the day. As the **Ohio** debate illustrates, categorical funding constraints can be addressed with innovative and coordinated responses.

Georgia

Georgia's universal early childhood education initiative serves all 4-year-olds in an effort to reduce high school dropout rates, teen pregnancy and crime.[34] Recognized as a component of Governor Zell Miller's comprehensive school reform effort targeting children from preschool to college age, the program has received high marks in a recent study. **Georgia**'s policymakers have expanded the state's prekindergarten program to focus on all 4-year-olds, regardless of family income, by earmarking state lottery funds.

With up to 4,000 children on waiting lists for the program in 1995, policymakers recognized that $180 million from lottery support was insufficient to serve all 4-year-olds. In 1996, over 16,000 additional prekindergarten slots were funded, resulting in a budget of approximately $205 million. Unlike any other state, **Georgia** offers free preschool to all 4-year-olds and parents are not required to contribute.

Established as a pilot program to serve 900 children in 1992-93 with $3 million, the preschool program has increased to 60,000 children in FY 1997. This is about 60 percent of **Georgia**'s 4-year-olds, and some of this

population is served by Head Start. Most of the expansion funding occurred when voters approved the lottery for education in the 1992 election. **Georgia** is the only state that earmarks lottery revenues to preschool. Now an evaluation of students two years after they completed the program indicates that participants are achieving higher academic skills and test scores than nonparticipants, they have better school attendance, and parents are more satisfied.[35]

The program has drawn national attention recently as a primary example of a renewed effort in the South to improve a perceived weak education ethic. Student achievement in the South had fallen behind national standards. But dramatic increases in early childhood education services in southern states such as **Georgia** may be changing that situation. Head Start enrollees in the South have increased by 65 percent since 1990, and state-funded preschool enrollees in the South have doubled since that time. According to the Southern Regional Education Board, half of all children enrolled in public preschool are in 15 Southern states.[36] In the past few years, legislatures in **Virginia** and **Tennessee** have authorized preschool programs.[37]

Georgia's programs operate out of public schools and licensed child care centers throughout the state. Each county has a local council to coordinate progress, but certain state standards apply. Programs must have family service coordinators, and children must receive basic health, dental, and nutrition services. The program offers parent-focused services, such as literacy or job training.[38] A ratio of one teacher for every 10 children is maintained, and lead teachers must have certain qualifications or professional credentials. Private programs are required to meet child care licensing standards set by the Department of Human Resources.[39]

School-age Child Care

Although increasing policy attention in recent years has focused on the care and education of preschoolers, caring for and educating children are responsibilities that extend far beyond age four. Care for older children is discussed in this chapter for two reasons: (1) state lawmakers are primary players in setting the state policy framework for school-age child care as part of their broader responsibility to examine overall child care and early education policy and (2) the public schools are assuming a major

TOP PRIORITY: PRESCHOOL PROGRAMS FOR AT-RISK KIDS

Publicly funded early childhood care and education historically have focused on programs for low-income children who are at risk of school failure. The most well-known program, Head Start, was created by Congress in 1965 to provide a variety of learning experiences to foster intellectual, social and emotional growth; encourage parental involvement; and provide necessary health and social services. Head Start programs operate in all 50 states and serve more than 700,000 children. In FY 1997, federal expenditures for Head Start programs are about $3.98 billion. Under both Democratic and Republican administrations, Head Start has recently been targeted for significant expansion. Legislatures in 13 states and D.C. supplement federal program funding as a simple policy strategy to increase the number of disadvantaged children with access to a comprehensive early childhood program.

role in supporting before- and after-school programs for school-age children.

The term "school-age child care"—also known as before- and after-school programs—refers to "formally organized services for 5- to 13-year-olds that occur before and/or after school during the academic year and all day when school is closed and parents are at work."[40]

Research suggests that self-care can be harmful compared with qualified organized programs, which produce more positive results. Reported harmful effects of self-care include susceptibility to peer pressure to engage in undesirable behavior, higher levels of fear and a greater number of troubling dreams at night. The beneficial effects of organized school-age child care programs include more highly developed social skills, better likelihood of forming friendships and improved reading and math scores.[41]

A 1988 survey of elementary school principals reported that "37 percent of principals sampled believe children would perform better in school if they weren't left unsupervised so long out of school."[42]

Research on School-age Child Care

Many children are alone during the hours before and after school. In the survey cited previously, 84 percent of school principals agreed that there is a need for before- and after-school programs.[43] These perceptions appear to be sound. According to the Census Bureau, as of 1991 approximately one-half the children under age 15 in the United States lived with mothers who worked, and two-

thirds of these children were grade-school age.[44] Though more than three-quarters of school-age children spent most of their time in school, many spent a significant amount of time caring for themselves when their mothers were working.[45]

A number of studies have found that school-age child care programs have resulted in positive outcomes for children and families. A 15-state evaluation of school-age child care programs for children ages 5 to 11 found better social and academic skills among participating students. Specific outcomes included reduced school vandalism, better homework quality, more interest in reading, improved grades, and better conflict management among at least a third of those studied.[46] Several studies reveal the importance of quality school-age child care on the lives of children. One documents "extensive positive effects for low-income children who attended formal after-school programs". It specifically found that low-income children in various school-age programs, compared with nonparticipants, had better grades and conduct in school, as well as better peer relations and emotional adjustment by the third grade.[47] Another study correlated leaving third graders alone after school with problem behavior. It also found that third and fifth graders spending unsupervised time with peers increased the likelihood of behavior problems.[48] One study found that these outcomes were more problematic for children living in proverty.[49] Quality of the programs was a significant factor in the effectiveness of the outcomes, particularly for low-income children in high-risk neighborhoods.[50]

Although the exact number of children in self-care is uncertain, officials at the Census Bureau estimate that about 4.6 million school-age children are in self-care, defined as being alone 25 hours or more weekly.[51] Moreover, the likelihood of self-care—as a latchkey child—increases with age. According to the bureau, fewer than 5 percent of children five to 11-years-old spent some time alone during their mother's work day, but by age 14 about one in five did so.[52]

Citizen concern over the numbers of unsupervised children is encouraging legislative action to support the creation of before- and after-school programs for older children and youth. As of spring 1991, an estimated 1.7 million children in kindergarten through eighth grade were regularly enrolled in before- and after-school programs.[53] Students attend programs offered by a variety of providers including public and private schools, city recreation departments, religious institutions, community centers and youth-serving agencies.[54]

It is estimated that public schools account for 28 percent of all school-age child care programs in the United States. In addition, of the total number of children in before- and after-school programs, 35 percent attend programs based in public schools.[55] Public school programs fall into two categories: programs operated by a school district and programs operated by private providers at a public school site. Programs are, in large part, available only to parents who can pay, since most are funded primarily by tuition.[56]

The Role of Public Schools

Opinions vary about the role of public schools in the provision of school-age child care. Those opposed tend to view these programs as extracurricular and, as such, outside the proper purview of public education, which should focus solely on academics. Opponents also contend that limited education resources are better devoted to basic education. Advocates for public school involvement argue that education extends beyond school hours and the academic calendar and that if education is to succeed in a modern world, public schools must do what many private schools already do—provide extended day programs for school-age children. Moreover, advocates point out that public school facilities are underutilized during nonschool hours, ought to be available to serve the public interest and have a pre-existing infrastructure that could be efficiently tapped for before- and after-school programs.

The role of public schools is further complicated by concerns over competition between existing private providers and public schools. Private providers worry that public school programs will hurt their business.

Many argue that since public school facilities are "paid for," public school programs operate with lower costs, putting private providers at a considerable competitive disadvantage. Furthermore, some argue that public school are actually less likely to provide appropriate care and that consumer choices should be available in the marketplace.

Whether school age child care programs are based in public schools, operated elsewhere by private providers or provided in collaboration between sectors is a debate that state legislators often face in deliberating state policy for school-age child care. Nonetheless, state legislative activity to support these programs is increasing.

State Legislative Action: School-age Child Care

Recent state legislative action related to school-age child care in public schools falls into three general areas: establishing school-age child care programs, authorizing the use of school facilities for school-age child care and licensing programs.

Program Establishment and Funding

As early as 1989, at least 14 states had appropriated state funds for school-age child care programs.[57] Before 1991, legislative activity reflected a small investment of state resources, primarily in grants for pilot programs. For example, the 1984 **New York** General Assembly appropriated $300,000 to start and expand school-age child care

SCHOOL READINESS: A NATIONAL GOAL

On the national level, new emphasis is being placed on the importance of quality early childhood experiences and their impact on the public school system. Goal 1 of the National Education Goals, established under the Bush administration and continued under the Clinton White House, states: "By the year 2000, all children in America will start school ready to learn"; thus the term school readiness. And in order for children to be prepared for school, access to high-quality and developmentally appropriate preschool programs for all disadvantaged and disabled children is called for in the Goals 2000 report. Congress has made school readiness a national priority by incorporating Goals 2000 into federal law and providing appropriations to assit states in achieving the goals.

programs, an amount which was doubled two years later. Although grants have been limited to $10,000, more than 200 programs proposing to create more than 10,000 new slots for school-age child care were funded in the program's first five years.[58] Though this state appropriation ended in 1990, **New York** leveraged federal child care funds for programs a few years later.[59]

In 1986, the **Maine** Legislature recognized that new providers of school-age child care had difficulty maintaining quality during their first year of operation. To address this issue, the Legislature created a fund to reimburse up to 25 percent of the first-year costs of running a program, with a cap of $10,000. The initial appropriation of $50,000 grew to $125,000 three years later.[60]

Hawaii's A+ School Age Child Care Program is among the nation's most comprehensive initiated by a state legislature. It is open to all children who are enrolled in public elementary schools, kindergarten through grade 6, in need of adult supervision after school. Other children eligible for this program include those who have been recommended by the school based on educational need.[61] In the 1996-97 school year, 26,400 students are expected to be served by A+ School-age Child Care in 177 programs located in public elementary schools.[62]

The purpose of the program, as defined in state statute, is to:

- provide affordable after-school supervision for children in a stimulating and caring environment;

- reinforce and expand learning for children by providing a range of activities including help with homework, reading, tutoring, enrichment in areas such as the arts and access to school libraries and classrooms;

- improve physical development by offering recreational and sports activities;

- increase the use of school facilities; and

- enhance the relationship between home and school by "collaboratively meeting the needs of children."

The Legislature appropriated $15 million to operate the A+ program for FY 1997.[63] School districts have the option of administering A+ programs or contracting with a private provider, but fees in either arrangement must be the same.[64] Of these programs, 123 were operated by the state, and 52 were operated privately in 1994.[65]

An evaluation conducted by the Wellesley College Center for Research on Women School-Age Child Care Project examined program characteristics and demographics, with the following findings:

1. Staff turnover rates are less than half the national average;

2. Average staff/student ratios (1:20) are better than the national average; and

3. Parental communication and participation is good.

The evaluation included a staff questionnaire to identify areas for program improvement. Staff-selected improvements were focused on the need for more training, additional resources for supplies and equipment and improvements in staffing levels, salaries and benefits.[66]

Other state legislatures also have established comprehensive state policies for school-age child care. **Indiana** requires public schools to provide programs for children in kindergarten through sixth grade. To help finance programs, **Indiana** created the School Age Child Care Project Fund with a tax on cigarettes sales. The fund generates approximately half a million dollars annually to leverage services for 3,000 children.[67] In **Delaware**, the state pays the school districts $50 per year for every child enrolled in a school-age child care program at a public school location. The legislature appropriated $200,000 for the fund.[68]

Texas created the School Child Care Services Fund to provide start-up costs for child care programs for school-age children before- and after-school and during holidays and vacations. The fund includes savings generated when state employees use federal dependent care spending accounts. As an employer, the state saves money because it does not have to provide Social Security contributions on the income that employees set aside in these accounts.[69]

Authorizing the Use of Public School Facilities

Since 1986, at least 17 state legislatures have authorized school districts to use school facilities to provide child care services either for school-age children or preschoolers.[70] Some state legislation outlines the respective responsibilities of public schools and other community-based providers for care of school-age children. As discussed earlier, **Hawaii** allows school districts discretion in offering programs or contracting for them. **Utah** and **South Carolina** specifically authorize school districts to contract with for-profit providers. **California** requires all plans for construction of new or modernized elementary school buildings to be designed to accommodate before- and after-school child care programs, according to need.[71]

A VIEW OF SCHOOLS OF THE FUTURE

Edward Zigler, one of the founders of Head Start, offers a vision of schools of the 21st century. His view encompasses an unprecedented level of family service delivery—including quality early education programs—at the nation's schools. Zigler's notion of comprehensive, family-friendly schools is being piloted in various forms across the nation. Zigler urges the expansion of the existing school system to provide before- and after-school care for children up to age 13, with full-day care on site for three-, four- and five-year-olds and other services depending on community needs. He points out that use of existing schools is an efficient option for meeting the nation's substantial, and growing, need for quality early care services.

Regulating Before- and After-school Programs

From 1986 to 1993, a dozen states had passed legislation to regulate school-age child care programs. These states are **California, Florida, Indiana, Iowa, Kansas, Maryland, Massachusetts, New York, Ohio, South Carolina, South Dakota**, and **Virginia**. Typically this legislation focuses on the administration of, and exemptions from, rules and regulations.

School-linked Social Services and Child Care

A promising area for the integration of both early childhood services and programs for school-age children is in the emerging area of school-linked or school-based social services. These services are designed to improve the educational performance and well-being of at-risk, school-age children by addressing their multiple needs in a coordinated manner in the public schools.[72] Social and health services are often termed school-based when provided on site and school-linked when otherwise arranged. The General Accounting Office reports that "at least eight states and more than 200 localities have developed school-linked services programs that deliver a variety of health, social, and education services at or near schools to students—many of whom are at risk of failing in school or dropping out."[73]

One example of school-based services is early care services offered at public schools for teen parents and their children. Every 67 seconds a baby is born to a teenager in the United States, and teen mothers are at high risk of dropping out of school.[74] Too often, teen moms also experience subsequent problems associated with academic failure, including underemployment, unemployment and welfare dependency. These phenomena indicate a unique need for child care among teen parents. One official noted, "Good child care is important not only because it allows these young women the opportunity to attend school, but also because it helps them gain parenting skills by encouraging them to participate in child development classes."[75] In addition, a study conducted for the U.S. Department of Health and Human Services (HHS) concludes that "teenage welfare mothers are much more likely to stay in school if they receive support services such as onsite child care."[76]

Some policymakers also see school-linked service delivery programs as efficient, cost-effective ways to link at-risk children and their families with prevention and early intervention services.[77] On-site child care for teen parents is one way to accomplish this.

State Legislative Initiatives: School-linked Child Care Services

Some states have enacted legislation to assist teen parents with child care needs. **California** initiated the idea of funding child care on or near high school and junior high school campuses in the 1980s.[78] In 1991, **Oregon** appropriated $1.5 million for grants to school districts for child development programs and teenage parent programs.[79] **Virginia** legislators approved a law in 1990 to authorize use of state or local funds by school boards to provide child care for teen parents enrolled in school.[80] **Iowa**'s 1992 family support legislation provides for a pilot project that includes all-day child care in school for parents of newborn infants.[81]

NEW WELFARE REQUIREMENTS AFFECT EDUCATION

The new federal welfare law, the Personal Responsibility and Work Opportunity Reconciliation Act of 1996, affects public schools' involvement in child care. It includes a number of provisions directed at teen parents on welfare, including requiring school participation and residence with an adult. Because of the school participation requirement for teen parents receiving federal welfare funds under the Temporary Assistance for Needy Families (TANF) block grant, states may wish to consider expanding school-based or near school child care services.

Good child care for teen parents is important for their education and self-sufficiency. With the goals of helping teen parents complete high school and learn good parenting skills, a number of states have tailored their child care programs specifically for teen parents. Examples include:

- Child care programs in public schools specifically for teen parents has been an approach taken by several states since the late 1980s. **California** and **Florida** are two examples of states that enacted laws to establish these programs.
- Family Resource Centers in schools provide a coordinated way for parents in school to access child care and other support services, such as parent education, health care, vocational training, tutoring and mentoring, counseling, housing and transportation. Several state legislatures, such as those in **Kentucky**, **Minnesota**, and **Iowa**, have authorized and funded these programs in the 1990s.

Educators will also face several other issues because of the new welfare law, including:

- Basic education for teen parents without a high school diploma;
- Vocational and school-to-work programs;
- Compensatory and special education for affected children;
- Food and nutrition services for children losing benefits;
- Health care services for children losing Medicaid;
- Transportation of student-mothers and their children;
- Certifying the satisfactory attendance of all student-parents;
- Determining citizenship/immigration status of children.[82]

Conclusion

Legislative education committees are examining early care and education, school-age child care and school-linked child care options more extensively because of the increasing numbers of mothers in the work force and the growing number of children in poverty.[83] Education systems are being called upon more and more often to address complex social problems that previously were handled in other settings or that did not exist. Considerable debate abounds regarding whether schools should expand their purview to take on more social service responsibility. Some argue that schools unfairly compete with an already existing service infrastructure that is better able to meet student and family needs.

Regardless of whether schools or other entities handle it, however, one thing is clear: students bring more to school than academic needs. And without dealing with their other needs, more and more students will fail to achieve their full academic potential.

CHAPTER 4

THE IMPLICATIONS OF EARLY CHILDHOOD SERVICES FOR JUVENILE JUSTICE

Introduction

Because of public perceptions that juvenile violence is increasing at alarming and unprecedented rates, juvenile justice is at the top of state legislative agendas across the country. Frequently, state juvenile justice policy is being deliberated in the glare of television cameras and intense constituent interest.

In the last two legislative sessions, 49 states and the **District of Columbia** together passed at least 617 enactments related to juvenile justice issues.[1] Recent legislative activity consists primarily of "get-tough" measures passed in response to perceptions that young people are behaving more violently, and data support at least some of those perceptions. But lawmakers are concerned that the legislative solutions demanded by their constituents to get tough on offenders will have little actual effect on public safety, while dramatically—and adversely—affecting state budgets.

Although state policymakers do not agree on solutions, some are turning to early childhood care and education to promote more effective, though longer term, answers. The best of these programs have shown to be remarkably effective— years later—in reducing both the incidence and the severity of criminal behavior among children who participated in them as preschoolers.

This chapter explores data regarding the scope and nature of juvenile violence, details fiscal considerations faced by lawmakers in promulgating institutional responses to juvenile crime, outlines the research base for alternative early intervention strategies and

discusses innovative state legislative initiatives to link early care and education with policy development in juvenile justice.

"There is a sense in this country that something has changed, that children are doing things that they didn't do before."

—Former Tennessee Representative Bill Purcell, House Majority Leader and chair of the state's Select Committee on Children and Youth, at a recent legislative hearing on juvenile justice

"The public perception is that kids have gone berserk and are out there killing people as never before, and we'd better do something about it yesterday."

—Former Tennessee Representative Karen Williams

The Scope of Juvenile Violence

In neighborhoods across the country, citizens are concerned about violence in their midst. Too often, they believe they are unsafe, even in their own homes, from random and vicious violent acts. Particularly in inner cities, mothers are afraid to let children play in their front yards, let alone public places like parks. Public concern that uncontrolled, violent juvenile gangs roam nearby extends beyond inner cities. Media reports of innocent bystanders, including children, being caught in the crossfire of gang violence fuel public fear of random violence.

EARLY CHILDHOOD INTERVENTIONS HELP PREVENT VIOLENCE

Early childhood programs can play a significant role in violence prevention. The American Psychological Association's Commission on Violence and Youth recommends that early childhood interventions directed toward parents, child care and health care providers be offered to help build the critical foundation of attitudes, knowledge and behavior related to aggression.[2]

Certain facts bear out public concerns. Juvenile arrests for violent crimes, for example, rose 67 percent in the decade between 1986 and 1995.[3] Furthermore, juvenile arrests for murder increased 90 percent, while arrests for aggravated assaults grew 78 percent during this same period.[4] Although shocking, these numbers must be viewed in context, some crime experts say.

The National Council on Crime and Delinquency notes that the higher number of juvenile arrests reflects the increased number of arrests in general. Juveniles actually made up a smaller proportion of overall arrests in 1992 than they did a decade earlier.[5] These statistics on juvenile crime run counter to current theories of criminology that hold that younger people are more likely to commit crimes than older people. In fact, juvenile offenders ages 10-17 currently account for a smaller percentage of violent offenders than their numbers in the U.S. population would predict.[6] Thus, young people are not driving the national crime wave but reflecting the overall violence in American society.

To say that youth crime and violence may not be more rampant than it was a decade ago, however, is not to say the problem can be ignored. As Del Elliott of the Center for the Study and Prevention of Violence points out, "Levels of youth participation in violent behavior are unacceptably high and constitute a serious crime and public health problem that must be addressed." Despite stable rates of total overall juvenile offenses, the most serious of them appear to be becoming more lethal and to involve younger and younger children. For example, the number of juvenile homicide offenders tripled between 1984 and 1994.[7] Some experts attribute these trends to the increased availability of firearms,[8] and data support the larger role of guns in incidents involving youngsters: four times as many juveniles were killed with a gun in 1994 than in 1984. The proportion of juvenile offenders who used a gun to commit homicide increased from 53 percent in 1983 to 82 percent in 1994.[9]

Barring more effective interventions, demographics suggest that the problem of juvenile violence is likely to increase, rather than subside, in coming years. The children of the baby boom generation are fast approaching their high-risk years for criminal behavior.

Cost Considerations in Juvenile Incarceration

Crime control is predominately a state and local function; states assume most correctional costs. These costs currently are escalating at unprecedented rates. In fact, adult corrections recently became the fastest growing segment of total state spending—overtaking Medicaid, the traditional budget buster.[10]

Overall, appropriations for adult corrections are taking an ever-larger bite out of state budgets. In FY 1997 these costs grew 6.2 percent, the largest increase of any state spending category.[11] Average state juvenile corrections budgets have risen even more dramatically, increasing by 17 percent from 1994 to 1995.[12] To operate its juvenile justice system each state spends an average of approximately $56 million annually, approximately $100 per juvenile per day in a locked facility.[13] Institutional costs for young offenders spill over into adult systems because states are turning over to adult systems increasing numbers of juveniles who commit serious offenses.

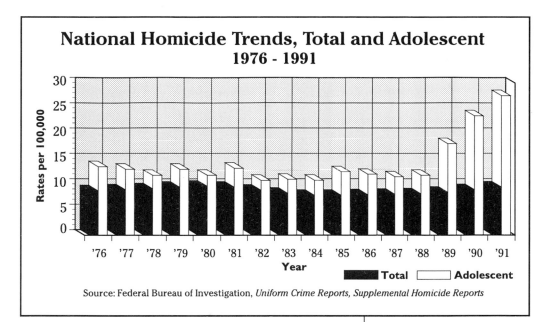

National Homicide Trends, Total and Adolescent
1976 - 1991

Source: Federal Bureau of Investigation, *Uniform Crime Reports, Supplemental Homicide Reports*

correctional institutions are there for nonviolent offenses. Furthermore, a 1993 analysis of 14 states concludes that nearly a third of juveniles housed in state training schools were considered appropriate for less secure—and less costly—settings.[15]

In addition, dealing with certain juveniles in more expensive adult correctional systems does not necessarily accomplish the purposes of better public safety and accountability. Del Elliott, principal investigator of the National Youth Survey, the country's most comprehensive violence research base, argues that there "is no clear evidence that increases in sentence length or confinement in adult institutions have any significant deterrent effect over shorter sentences and confinement in juvenile institutions."[16] Furthermore, juveniles transferred to the adult court do not receive harsher penalties than they would have in the juvenile system, despite policymakers' intention to hold them more accountable for serious crimes within adult systems.[17] Other researchers note that most juveniles waived to adult court are not sentenced for serious violent offenses, or even crimes against persons.[18] Unfortunately, these facts are not widely known.

These costs concern state budget analysts because operational costs for incarceration are inflexible, affecting budget projections far into the future. This is because, once established, incarceration policies are generally not rolled back and each criminal sentence requires a commitment of future state resources; in addition, states must meet certain legal standards in operating prison systems. As states add more incarceration facilities, state revenue available for other purposes, including education or services for families and the elderly, is effectively reduced. And besides the high cost of incarceration and of transferring youths to the adult system, there is evidence that these approaches are not effective.

In contrast, alternatives to incarceration are promising. Seven separate studies show reduced rates of recidivism for juvenile offenders placed in alternatives to institutionalization. Furthermore, the National Council on Crime and Delinquency attributes **Massachusetts'** low juvenile offense recidivism rates—and $11 million a year savings—partly to its extensive use of community-based care instead of locked facilities.[14] Currently, more than half the juveniles in youth

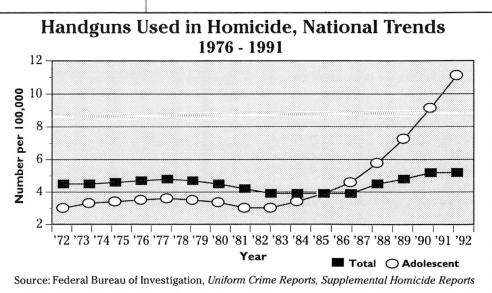

Handguns Used in Homicide, National Trends
1976 - 1991

Source: Federal Bureau of Investigation, *Uniform Crime Reports, Supplemental Homicide Reports*

An increasing body of research evidence suggests that intervening even earlier with alternatives that encompass quality early care and education programming is more cost-effective in the longer term.[19] For example, the longitudinal cost-benefit analysis of the High/Scope Perry Preschool program suggests that quality early childhood education can directly reduce crime costs. Researchers concluded that "the estimated effect of the preschool program is to reduce the costs of crime by $148,714 per program participant over a lifetime."[20] This includes savings in costs to victims and to the criminal justice system, adjusted for inflation. In 1992, researchers estimated that the cost savings already totaled $70,000 per program participant. Other studies of early care and education programs, discussed later in the chapter, found similar results.

> "Compared to past years, this cohort of adolescents consists of a higher proportion of youngsters who have been reared in extreme poverty, exposed to dangerous drugs, and physically abused. Every predictable indicator of violence is against this generation."
>
> —Barry Krisberg, President
> National Council on Crime and Delinquency

Still, so-called "get-tough" approaches are increasingly popular with a constituency concerned about its welfare and safety. Given these public perceptions, legislators face two problems. First, since constituents are demanding immediate answers, they must choose among short-term solutions that vary in their effectiveness in remediating juvenile violence. Too often, effective options supported by the research to build a diverse continuum of juvenile justice services are not well accepted by a public demanding more punitive, institutional responses. Second, lawmakers must also balance effective long-term policy with constituent demands for these immediate solutions. Increasingly, lawmakers are attempting to address public safety concerns with greater emphasis on prevention and early intervention alternatives. Among the most promising options to date incorporate quality early childhood care and education programs that have a proven track record in reducing subsequent juvenile crime and violence.

Research on Prevention and Early Intervention

Those who study juvenile crime say that the highest rates of participation in serious violence occur around the ages of 16-17 years.[21] Consequently, criminologists argue, the key to preventing violence is to affect children's lives well before they reach later adolescence. Longitudinal studies of quality early childhood services support this approach, verifying that exposure to quality early childhood programs reduce at-risk children's later involvement in criminal behavior.

Evidence from the High/Scope Perry Preschool Project study indicates that early childhood education can reduce low-income children's prospects for later involvement with the criminal justice system. Studies conducted when those who had participated in the preschool program reached age 19 and again when they were age 27 showed lower delinquency and arrest rates for the preschool participants.[22] By age 27, 58 percent of program participants had been arrested, compared with an arrest rate of 69 percent for a control group. More striking is the comparison of frequent offenders, who had been arrested five or more times. Seven percent of the program participants were in this category, but 35 percent of nonparticipants were frequent offenders.[23]

Other studies have also documented the effect of quality early care and education programs on juvenile criminal behavior. The Syracuse University Family Development Research Program provided child care and home visits to very poor, mostly black families. "Longitudinal research showed that only 6 percent of the program children, compared to 22 percent of the control children, had been processed as adolescent probation cases."[24] In this study, control group children committed more serious delinquent acts, such as robbery, physical and sexual assault and burglary. The study found that "the average juvenile justice cost per child was $186 for the preschool home visiting group and $1,985 for the control group."[25]

Another program, a Houston, Texas, Parent-Child Development Center offers center-based child care for one- and two-year-olds and early childhood and parenting education to their parents. A study of this program revealed that when the children reached ages eight to 11,

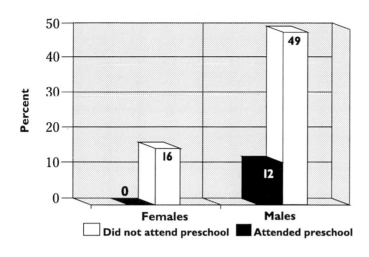

Five or More Lifetime Arrests by Age 27, by Preschool Experience and Gender

Source: Schweinhart et al., *Significant Benefits*

teachers rated children who had participated in the intervention as more social, engaging in less problem and disruptive behavior, including fighting.[26]

Although it is not entirely clear why early childhood care and education works, quality programs mitigate some of the primary and interrelated risk factors that researchers have associated with a greater propensity for delinquency and crime: school failure, economic distress and abuse and neglect.[27]

A March 1994 study by the Office of Juvenile Justice and Delinquency Prevention of three urban areas maintains that school performance, whether measured by reading achievement or by being held back in the same grade, relates to delinquency. It showed that in Pittsburgh, Pa., students with higher reading achievement had lower delinquency rates. The study concludes that over time commitment to school reduces delinquency. In Denver, Colo., the study showed that 30 percent of juveniles with low school commitment were delinquent, compared with only 12 percent with high commitment to school. This trend was repeated in Pittsburgh and in Rochester, N.Y.[28]

Other research links adult criminal behavior with economic factors. A 1991 U.S.

Department of Justice study of recent U.S. Census data indicates that a state prison inmate is four times more likely than average to have been unemployed during the month before his arrest and nearly twice as likely to have earned under $10,000 in the year before his arrest.[29]

An increasing body of research suggests that violence is learned through exposure to it, often in a family setting. A 1994 study that followed 1,000 seventh and eighth-grade students for four years found that mistreated youngsters who grew up in violent families were twice as likely to commit brutal acts as were children from nonviolent families. The highest rates of youth violence occurred among youngsters exposed to all three types of family violence—spouse abuse, child mistreatment and general hostility. Nearly 80 percent of these youngsters reported involvement in violent delinquency.[30] Del Elliott's research points out that a child who has either been abused or witnessed such behavior is 40 percent more likely to be violent as an adolescent.[31] In research sponsored by the National Institute of Justice, Cathy Spatz Widom documented that "being abused or neglected as a child increased the likelihood of arrest as a juvenile by 53 percent."[32] Several studies by Dorothy Otnow Lewis also confirm that a history of abuse or family violence is a predictor of future violence.[33]

JOBS AND CRIME

Another deterrent to crime is the availability of jobs for the nation's most vulnerable populations. Del Elliott's longitudinal research shows that high chronic unemployment rates in disorganized neighborhoods results in illegitimate labor markets and violence. Sociologist William Julius Wilson's studies of selected census tracts in Chicago, published as *The Truly Disadvantaged: The Inner City, The Underclass and Public Policy*, suggest that an unprecedented "underclass" is being created in inner-city neighborhoods, where virtually no legitimate economic opportunities exist for residents to aspire to—leaving welfare and crime as the major life options.

VIOLENCE GENERATES MORE VIOLENCE

According to the American Psychological Association's (APA) Commission on Violence and Youth, "the strongest developmental predictor of a child's involvement in violence is a history of previous violence." The commission's 1993 report asserts that violence factors "are alterable, especially at the earliest stages of child development. For this reason, effective intervention for aggressive and violent behavior in childhood is critical, and the earlier the better." The APA mentions inconsistent and physically abusive parental discipline as one of the violent behavior patterns that contribute to later antisocial behavior.

Because high-quality early childhood services specifically affect children's prospects in some of the primary risk areas, it is speculated that these benefits also translate into a reduced propensity toward antisocial behavior, including delinquency and adult crime. The following section details research on the effects of quality early childhood programs on certain risk factors associated with violence. These include school and economic performance and the incidence of abuse and neglect among participating children and their families.

The Effect of Early Childhood Programs on the Propensity Toward Violence

With regard to school performance, the most recent High/Scope follow-up study of the Perry preschoolers indicates that good early childhood programs lead to consistent improvement in elementary and secondary school achievement as well as to increased rates of postsecondary enrollments. Two-thirds of the program participants had graduated from high school, compared with less than half of the control group.[34] More details regarding education results from the High/Scope Perry Preschool program are outlined in chapter 3.

Data from the High/Scope Perry Preschool study also show that quality preschool can contribute to greater economic self-sufficiency. At age 19, 50 percent of the program group, compared with 32 percent of the control group, held jobs. Forty-five percent of the program group, compared with 25 percent of the control group, supported themselves or were supported by a spouse. Furthermore, 18 percent of the program group, compared with 32 percent of the control group, were on welfare at age 19.[35] In addition, the most recent evidence of the High/Scope Perry Preschool Project indicates that at age 27—or over 20 years later—program participants not only had higher earnings, but also had fewer members who had received social services in the previous 10 years. Specifically, the study for participants at age 27 indicates that, compared with a control group, the program group had higher

- monthly and annual earnings ($1,219 vs. $766/month);
- employment rates (71 percent vs. 59 percent); and
- home ownership rates (36 percent vs. 13 percent).[36]

Some early childhood programs also have documented success in reducing the incidence of abuse and neglect. Among the most notable is the Healthy Start Program, first initiated in Hawaii in 1985. This home-visiting program for new moms targets families who exhibit certain risk factors associated with child abuse and neglect. Among other components, the program provides parent education regarding child development and certain health-related services for newborns. Evaluations of this program show significant reductions in child abuse and neglect. Furthermore, only 0.5 percent of the program participants reported incidents of child abuse or neglect.[37] This compares with confirmed abuse and neglect in 2.7 percent of high-risk families who did not participate in Healthy Start.[38] Results from the **Hawaii** program have prompted other states to follow Hawaii's lead. Legislatures in **Florida, Iowa, Ohio, Oregon, Tennessee** and **Washington**, for example, have recently initiated programs.

Other early care and education programs have shown similar promise in reducing child abuse and neglect. For example, in Elmira, N.Y., the Prenatal/Early Infancy Project found fewer cases of child abuse among at-risk mothers who had received nurse home-visiting services than among similar mothers who had not.[39]

State Legislative Initiatives: Early Childhood and Juvenile Justice

Recently, several state legislatures deliberated early childhood initiatives under the auspices of their juvenile violence prevention packages. State approaches varied:

- **Minnesota** proponents attempted to balance—dollar for dollar—"get-tough" options with prevention strategies;

- The **Washington** legislature approved an overall reorganization of the children's service system to focus on community-based remediation of risk factors associated with violence;

- The influential **Tennessee** Joint Select Committee on Children and Youth took a proactive approach: holding public hearings before the regular session designed to educate both legislators and the public about the links between early care and education and youth violence prevention;

- In 1993, **Colorado** created a youthful offender system, separate from both the adult and juvenile justice systems, and the following year prevention proponents were successful in demanding an increased state investment in early intervention.

The **Delaware** General Assembly used yet another approach: garnering support for a separate early childhood initiative by linking it with violence prevention. In authorizing the state early childhood education program for poor children, the General Assembly cited the state's Criminal Justice Council as endorsing early intervention strategies as one long-term solution for juvenile delinquency.[40] The **Delaware** legislature appropriated $900,000 for the first year of this new program, $1.4 million for the second year and nearly $1.8 million for the third year.[41]

Such legislative strategies have resulted in a variety of prevention initiatives in the states. An increasing number include early care and education programs. About half of the $13.9 million appropriated in **Minnesota**'s 1994 omnibus juvenile justice proposal was earmarked for prevention. Funds are included for learning readiness programs and home instruction programs for preschoolers, as well as for expanding community crime reduction programs, reducing gang involvement and making

grants for school-based violence prevention.[42]

Colorado's prevention initiatives include a $19.4 million state preschool program that serves 8,500 at-risk 4-year-olds, nearly twice the number of children served previously. The preschool funding level was more than twice the amount appropriated two years earlier. The state also spends $1 million for family development center grants and $7 million for youth crime prevention and intervention grants.[43] In 1996, the state legislature earmarked 20 percent of the these funds for programs for children under age 9.[44]

Iowa's 1994 juvenile justice legislation includes early intervention and school-based violence prevention efforts. The package includes $1.8 million for early intervention, $4 million to expand supervisory programs through the state Department of Public Health, including school-based probation services. Legislators allocated $2 million to expand school services focusing on early intervention and prevention, based on a **New Jersey** model.[45]

Despite the increased level of attention to violence prevention, in all states most fiscal resources are still devoted to reacting to crime after the fact, focusing on punishment and incarceration. But as the following case studies in **Tennessee, North Carolina** and **Washington** indicate, some innovative lawmakers are expanding the policy debate to include consideration of the long-term implications of prevention and early intervention.

Tennessee

For nine years the **Tennessee** legislature has been on the cutting edge of children's reform initiatives, largely because of the leadership of its influential Joint Select Committee on Children and Youth. In 1994, the committee conducted extensive hearings on youth violence and crime prevention.

THE RELATIONSHIP BETWEEN INCOME AND DELINQUENCY

The American Psychological Association report *Violence and Youth: Psychology's Response* confirms that "it is the combination of poverty, inequality and lack of access to resources that are the most consistent predictors" of violence. The August 1993 report recommends home visitor programs for at-risk families and preschool programs that address children's intellectual, emotional and social needs, among other prevention strategies.

In the wake of these hearings, the General Assembly approved measures to increase accountability for serious juvenile offenders, but also approved major initiatives anchored in successful early childhood programs. In developing and recommending passage of the Early Childhood Development Act of 1994, the committee focused legislative attention on early childhood intervention as one important key to preventing crime and addressing its root causes.[46]

In addition, the committee used its "bully pulpit" to begin a process of citizen education. Building on constituent interest in juvenile crime and violence, the committee, chaired by children's advocate and then House Majority Leader Bill Purcell, scheduled a two-day public hearing in December 1993, before the legislative session. Media packed the chamber as the committee heard testimony from juvenile court judges, juvenile corrections administrators, academicians and others. In addition to hearing from corrections experts, a full day of the public hearing was reserved to consider "the state of the art" in prevention.

After considering a number of early childhood program models, the committee endorsed a multifaceted prevention strategy that included the following:

• Creation of a state Healthy Start program modeled after Hawaii's to prevent child abuse and neglect;

• Development of a plan by the state education agency to provide early childhood education services to at-risk three- and four-year-olds to ensure school success;

• Doubling the number of school-linked family resource centers; and

• Expansion of family preservation services to meet statewide needs.

The proposed package passed overwhelmingly during the 1994 session because of the influence of committee members and the positive media coverage generated at the hearings. The state's crime package also allowed transfer to adult court of children under age 14 who commit certain violent acts, prohibited handgun possession by juveniles and increased penalties for crimes on school property.[47] But the committee's

presession work brought longer-term prevention options to the General Assembly's agenda, as well. This "carrot-and-stick" strategy improved the prevention initiatives' chances for passage. Former House Majority Leader Bill Purcell, the bill's sponsor, explained: "We made it easier to prosecute these cases and expedite the number of children tried as adults. Second, we significantly increased our efforts to help children avoid becoming criminals, which was our first comprehensive legislation dealing with early intervention."[48]

SMART START IN NORTH CAROLINA

North Carolina's 1994 juvenile crime prevention package built upon its two-year, $67 million early childhood initiative enacted a year earlier. The Smart Start program currently provides funding for 47 community-based early care and education programs in 55 counties. Championed by both the executive and legislative branches, Smart Start is intended for expansion to a statewide program. In describing Smart Start, the North Carolina Department of Human Resources wrote, "Every dollar spent now on early childhood education will save more than $7.00 down the road in remedial education, welfare, prisons, and crime." The legislature has also specifically targeted funds for at-risk child care services, specifying that "these programs shall include juvenile delinquency prevention programs and services designed to prevent youth suicide" (see chapter 8 for more information about the Smart Start program).

North Carolina

Reflecting intense constituent interest, several state legislatures have recently convened special sessions to deal with crime—**North Carolina, Colorado, Florida** and **Utah**. Called by Governor James Hunt, the seven-week session in **North Carolina** in 1994 considered both punitive measures and early childhood prevention options. As in **Tennessee**, legislators in **North Carolina** expanded the number of children who could be transferred to the adult court and increased firearm penalties. The legislature also approved the governor's request to enact a so-called "three strikes" bill, which requires life in prison without parole for people convicted of three violent felonies.[49]

The legislature was successful in expanding the governor's crime-control agenda to include significant investments in prevention and early care programs. During the session, the General Assembly appropriated $37 million for prevention services anchored specifically in early childhood, family and school programs designed to reduce crime and violence at its roots.[50] These measures built upon the foundation of a comprehensive early care and education initiative previously approved by the legislature under the governor's leadership. The crime prevention package includes several components:

- Family resource centers funding is approximately $2 million for 1996-97. In a recent report, the centers have shown to be instrumental in helping children prepare for academic success, bringing communities together, advancing job preparedness, and helping with the transition from public assistance to employment.[51] The legislation targets services to neighborhoods that have disproportionately high levels of children at risk of school or social failure, low-income families and crime and juvenile delinquency.[52] The Division of Family Development tries to coordinate the grants with Smart Start, the early childhood initiative. The program awards grants to collaborative agencies made up of schools, private councils, social services and health organizations and community-based groups.[53]

- A $6 million appropriation for after-school activities for children in kindergarten to age 9. Sixty-four agencies have grants under the Support Our Students (SOS) program. A North Carolina Central University evaluation found that the SOS program had good results, such as better grades, fewer dropouts, and improved student behavior and attitudes.[54] The program primarily assists collaborative community-based programs that provide meaningful after-school activities for at-risk students.[55] The department has awarded SOS grants to 53 agencies, ranging from community action and development groups to YMCAs and YWCAs.[56]

- A $30 million appropriation for juvenile crime intervention and prevention grants as well as additional school staff to assist students at risk of school failure. The legislation links these program dollars with school-based resource centers and after-school programs, as well as with implementation of locally designed initiatives to serve at-risk students and their families and to minimize violent student behavior.[57] The $30 million was rolled into a larger At-Risk Student Services/Alternative Schools fund in 1995. This $93.9 million fund includes services for dropouts, summer school instructional and remediation support, drug and alcohol prevention, preschool screening, and safe schools.[58]

Washington

Washington's 1994 youth violence prevention initiative represents a more exhaustive, broad-based approach. In short, the Legislature attempted to fuse social science research and theory into comprehensive state policy. Using a risk-focused prevention model developed by University of Washington sociologist David Hawkins, the legislature established a new local structure to coordinate services for children. The legislation establishes broad-based community networks to assess local needs, based on a review of public health data and examination of risk factors such as dropout rates, availability of drugs and guns and community disorganization. After this extensive analysis, the networks are expected to develop a plan for local service delivery that will address the risk factors and reduce or remediate conditions that place children and youth at risk of dysfunction—including violence and delinquency.

The original legislation also allows for pooling a variety of state funding streams—including early care and intervention services—to allow block grants to the networks to achieve their local reform plans.

Approximately $10.8 million was appropriated for the community networks for 1995-97; $8.4 million is from federal Family Preservation and Support Act funds and approximately $2.4 million from new "sin" taxes. $7.5 million was proposed for community networks for the 1997-99 biennium.[59] Currently, the networks are explicitly authorized to fund any program that reflects locally established priorities. For example, they may fund programs like home-visiting to prevent abuse and neglect; parenting skill training and family support services are also specified for funding to complement home-visiting. Networks may also use funds for organizational development and planning. Further, the legislation contains a school-age child care component, allowing the networks to include matching grants to school districts in their comprehensive plans. These grants are intended to support expanded use of school facilities for after-hours recreational opportunities and day care.[60]

The law also authorizes the state Family Policy Council—made up of top state officials from health, human services, employment and economic development agencies—to provide training and technical assistance to the networks and to approve each network's plan. The council and the networks must report by

January 1 of each year to the governor and the legislature about the feasibility of decategorizing state funds for local programs and to determine which funds are appropriate for pooling. These funding streams, specified in the legislation, include child care, early intervention and educational services, early childhood education, Head Start, Readiness to Learn, foster care, crisis residential care and family preservation and support services.[61]

As in other states, this type of financing reform is being considered to remove perverse incentives in the state financing structure that seem to favor institutional and crisis services, rather than prevention and earlier intervention. The proposed reform, however, is not without controversy among some providers and advocates, who question whether adequate time is provided for capacity-building among local networks to effectively assess risk factors and develop adequate local service-delivery plans. Since network regions were not determined until September 1994, legislative observers anticipate that most will not pursue the decategorization option for some time.[62]

Conclusion

Today, crime and violence—particularly that associated with youth—are major concerns of voters. Increasingly, however, legislators are discovering that past approaches are not working to increase public safety and stem violence. Across the country, state lawmakers are examining the evaluation research on prevention and early care and intervention to inform their decisions on juvenile justice policy. Most initiatives to date, are experimental and somewhat piecemeal, as lawmakers test the efficacy of different approaches. The experience and data provided by such state pilot projects are important because they will influence violence prevention and punishment policy in the future. Research shows that early intervention can interrupt the cycle of violence; that community-based responses can be more effective than costly incarceration and that violence is associated with risk factors like child abuse and school failure which are preventable. The actions by state lawmakers must take to fashion effective solutions are two-pronged. First, they must "get smart" as well as "get tough" by choosing among short-term policies that have shown to be effective in the research. Second, they must balance constituent

demands for immediate responses with the need to implement longer-term solutions, including early childhood care and education programs.

On many levels, however, research on violence is just beginning. For example, states are just beginning to look at exposure to violence and its effect on children and youth. An increasing number of children are growing up in violent environments in which they witness or experience violence at earlier ages.[63] In 1992, homicide became the second leading cause of death among teens.[64] Intervention is being explored in some jurisdictions as evidence mounts that, for many children, "involvement in aggression and violence follows a life course trajectory that starts as early as three- or four-years-old."[65] The risk factors associated with violent behavior are complex and interrelated and include, according to the current research, economic deprivation, abuse and neglect, school failure, community disorganization, substance abuse, among many other factors. But much of the important research discussed in this chapter suggests that violence is not intractable: prevention can work, but its cost-benefits are realized over the long term. And as a recent report from the National Governors' Association points out, it is a generally held belief that "intervention should begin early, and programs should be comprehensive and long term."[66]

CHAPTER 5

THE ROLE OF EARLY CHILDHOOD CARE IN HEALTH POLICY

Introduction

State legislators grappling with health care reform soon recognize that child health, particularly the health and nutrition of young children, is a cornerstone of health care cost containment. Good health is key to children's development, to their future personal and social development and their success in school and, later, in work.

A considerable body of research attests to the cost-benefits of adequate primary care and preventive medicine, particularly during pregnancy and in children's early years. This research contributed to development of state legislative health initiatives to expand medical care to more poor pregnant women and their children. State legislatures in **Alabama, Illinois, Indiana, Iowa, Maryland, Minnesota, Mississippi, Missouri, New Jersey, New York, Pennsylvania, Tennessee** and **Texas** initiated such programs before the mandated federal expansions of Medicaid coverage for these populations in 1989.

A major issue in the health care reform debate is providing preventive and primary care to the uninsured. These ranks include approximately 8.4 million children for whom the lack of routine well-child health services too frequently results in preventable disabilities or conditions that demand greater public expenditures for expensive medical care and remedial services later.[1]

State and federal programs too frequently address separate aspects of healthy child development. But children's needs for nutrition, health care, child care and education are interrelated; and state legislators are beginning to conceptualize policy development in terms of the whole child. Such thinking, however, challenges the traditional ways that legislators create and fund government programs and hold them accountable. And even though more legislators are considering more systemic approaches, to date there are few policy models, particularly in creating statutory linkages between health care and early childhood services.

In the spirit of innovation, this chapter challenges legislators to think creatively about ways in which early childhood care and education can be integrated with health care initiatives. (Also see chapter 8 on family support for further discussion of comprehensive program models.)

> "Preventive health services are especially important for young children, as illness and handicaps not treated in childhood can easily become barriers to achievement in school and in society."
>
> U.S. Department of Health and Human Services
> *EPSDT: A Guide for Educational Programs*

Health and Caregiving: The Research

A variety of benefits result from better access to health care including lower mortality and morbidity, fewer visits to specialists, fewer emergency room visits and lower hospitalization rates.[2] A New York City study of low-income children and adolescents studied the effects of using a primary care model in which comprehensive health care and linkages to a health and social services network was offered consistently by providers. This research found fewer and less severe health problems, more comprehensive early medical care, timely immunizations, better health knowledge and practices by mothers, fewer injuries, greater likelihood of becoming enrolled in the Women, Infants and Children program (WIC), and greater likelihood of eating regular meals.[3]

Furthermore, research in specific areas, including immunizations and good prenatal care, indicates notable cost benefits. In a recent study published by the *Journal of the American Medical Association*, researchers estimate that a vaccination program to prevent chicken pox saves society more than $5 for every $1 invested.[4] Another major study confirms the economic benefits of haemophilus influenzae type b immunization to prevent meningitis.[5] Almost a decade ago, the Institute of Medicine estimated that "for every $1 spent for prenatal care for high-risk women, $3.38 would be saved in the total cost of caring for low birthweight infants requiring expensive care."[6] Research also indicates that a lack of adequate health care during the early years can result in developmental delays and disabilities that increase special education costs.

Good health care, nutrition and environment influence human development from conception into adulthood. In 1991, the Carnegie Corporation convened the Task Force on Meeting the Needs of Young Children to examine the current base of scientific knowledge pertaining to the healthy development of young children and to formulate policy recommendations based on this evidence. Following more than two years of deliberation by the multidisciplinary task force, its report Starting Points concludes, "We don't have to guess about the benefits of early health care; indeed, in no other area of social policy can costs and benefits be calculated so precisely. For example, every dollar spent on childhood immunizations saves $10 in later medical costs."[7] (See the box "Early Health Care Is Important" for other examples.)

Research thus confirms the importance of both health factors and caregiving—including parenting and

EARLY HEALTH CARE IS IMPORTANT

- In 1992, rates of immunization against common childhood diseases among two-year-olds were only 30 percent in some states; in most states, they were below 60 percent.

- Up to 45 percent of low birthweight babies experience learning difficulties.

- In the United States, nine out of every 1,000 infants die before age one—a mortality rate higher than that of 19 other nations.

- A longitudinal study in **Hawaii** found that "when children with a variety of prenatal health problems grew up in families that were both poor and dysfunctional, they more often showed later antisocial behaviors such as truancy and delinquency."

- Children growing up in poverty suffer from higher rates of malnutrition and anemia than other children. In one urban hospital, low-income two-year-olds were 40 percent more likely than other toddlers to be severely underweight and clinically malnourished. They were 60 percent more likely to suffer malnutrition in the winter months when, researchers speculated, families diverted their limited funds from food to fuel.

- The influence of early environment on brain development is long-lasting. One group of inner-city children was exposed, from early infancy, to good nutrition, toys and playmates; a second group was raised in less stimulating settings. The positive factors had a measurable impact on brain function at 12 years of age and an even greater effect by age 15, suggesting that the benefits of early intervention are cumulative.

—Carnegie Corporation of New York
Starting Points: Meeting the Needs of Our Youngest Children

child care—on healthy child development. Considering that 53 percent of mothers now return to work within a year of a child's birth, public policies around the quality of care provided to infants and young children take on even greater significance.[8] Successful child development depends on the environment in which a child spends his or her time; and for increasing numbers of infants and toddlers, this place is a child care setting for much of the day.

Healthy child development encompasses both prenatal and postnatal stages and includes consideration of the interrelationships among good nutrition, adequate and timely health care and safe, nurturing environments. State and federal lawmakers have responded to these needs by creating and funding programs targeted to the "years before school." Federal expenditures in 1993 targeted for the 15 largest such programs totaled $21 billion. Of this amount, 45 percent was allocated for health programs, 35 percent for education and 20 percent for nutrition.[9] The most well known of these programs include Medicaid expansions to cover more children and pregnant women, the WIC nutrition program and Head Start.

Coordination of Early Childhood Programs With Health Services

As part of the movement to reinvent government, initiatives have been proposed to integrate human service delivery systems to make them more humane and more effective as well as more efficient. Reform efforts seek to institutionalize systems of care that are truly flexible and responsive to the real and interacting needs of consumers—children and their families.

Within this context, coordination of health and early childhood care services makes sense—particularly with respect to services for low-income populations. And given the increasing numbers of working parents, the early care and education infrastructure offers an exciting potential for moving toward more widely available family support

services. Some potential areas for coordination include

- prenatal, postnatal and well-baby care;
- child health screening;
- nutrition programs; and
- parent education.

Most often linkages are achieved through statutory requirements or interagency agreements to provide services either at the site of an early childhood program or at a health clinic.

Early childhood programs provide a natural setting for health care providers to connect with infants, young children and their parents, including pregnant mothers. The most well known and successful example of providing health services to children enrolled in early childhood programs can be found in voluntary arrangements between Medicaid and Head Start. Performance standards

COORDINATING HEALTH AND CHILD CARE AT THE LOCAL LEVEL

A considerable amount of activity to coordinate health and early childhood services occurs locally. For example, a 1993 survey of 139 maternal and child health programs operated by large, urban public health departments found extensive linkages between Head Start and the Maternal and Child Health Programs. Eighty-eight percent of urban health departments surveyed reported some involvement with Head Start programs. Of 11 cities with populations over 500,000, only one jurisdiction reported no involvement with Head Start. The most frequent collaborative services reported were (1) physicals; Early and Periodic, Screening, Diagnostic, and Treatment (EPSDT); or other periodic assessments (53 percent); (2) screenings for hearing, vision, lead, anemia or dental problems (44 percent); and (3) immunizations (41 percent). In terms of governance, 45 percent of respondents reported that a representative of the local health department serves on a Head Start board of directors, policy committee or health advisory committee. Moreover, over half of the respondents reported a very good working relationship with Head Start. Specific examples of local coordination included

- The Head Start program in Columbus, Ohio, contracts with the local health department for a nurse who coordinates the program's health component;

- The public health agency in Orange County, Calif., arranges services for Head Start children for whom abnormalities are identified as part of EPSDT examinations; and

- The city of Madison, Wis., is planning to co-locate Head Start with a community health center, Planned Parenthood and the public library.[10]

for Head Start have required a health component from the program's inception, a fact that explains the program's progress in linking participants with health services. Though Medicaid is not legally required to contract with other agencies, the two entities have been collaborating for years to coordinate services.

Coordinating services addresses both organizational efficiency and effectiveness. Collaborative arrangements use existing infrastructures, while overcoming barriers that discourage or prevent eligible children and families from receiving essential medical services. Thus, early childhood programs can provide eligibility information to families about public health programs or provide services, such as Medicaid enrollment or immunizations, on site. Such services help solve such problems as lack of information and transportation, long waiting lines and inconvenient hours at public clinics.

Several states offer examples of coordination. In **Louisiana, Kansas and Idaho,** nurses work as consultants to child care programs. **Oregon** has also conducted many joint health and child care programs.[11] Public health clinics are also beginning to address the special needs of children. **Florida, Louisiana, South Carolina** and **Texas** provide child care services for patients' children during health care visits.[12]

Federal Laws That Promote Coordination

Areas of federal law that provide an opportunity for states to coordinate health and early childhood services for selected populations include the following:

- **Medicaid.** Medicaid covered 17.2 million children in 1994.[13] These children are generally recipients of the former AFDC program or Supplemental Security Insurance (SSI). In addition, Medicaid covers certain low-income children and pregnant women who do not receive public assistance, a category known as "Medicaid Only." EPSDT can provide screening and follow-up health services for these children. Once eligible for Medicaid, children qualify for EPSDT. Because Medicaid requires states to conduct outreach services to inform potentially eligible populations about the program, early childhood programs and EPSDT are good candidates for program coordination. Furthermore, federal guidelines strongly encourage or require EPSDT coordination with other programs.[14]

- **The Family Preservation and Support Act.** A new subsection of the federal Adoption Assistance and Child Welfare Act, this program allots to states up to $930 million dollars between 1993 and 1998 to provide additional services to support families and to preserve families in crisis. Specifically targeted in the legislation are "services designed to improve parenting skills with respect to matters such as child development, family budgeting, coping with stress, health and nutrition." The U.S. Department of Health and Human Services has encouraged states to use the new funding to leverage collaborative, interagency systems reform. Consequently, states have been directed to use the first year's allocation (ending October 1995) in developing five-year strategic plans for reform.

In an effort to further collaboration between federal agencies, the Public Health Service has earmarked an additional $50,000 in Maternal and Child Health Bureau (MCH) funds for states to work with the state Title V MCH program to incorporate a health component, with an emphasis on home-visiting services, within each state's required five-year plan. This planning process poses a unique opportunity to link early care, health and other child welfare services. Both lawmakers and early care providers should be involved. Information about the process and the developing plans can be obtained from the state child welfare agency that administers the new federal funding stream.[15]

- **Maternal and Child Health Services Block Grant (MCHBG).** Authorized under Title V of the Social Security Act, the MCHBG provides states with funds to promote the health of all women, children, and youth, including children with special health care needs. The program concentrates on those with low incomes or limited access to care. In addition to the block grant, the federal Maternal and Child Health Bureau also funds several discretionary grant programs. The bureau places high priority on coordinating services by encouraging "one-stop shopping," defined as "any local service system of integrated services delivery, where women and children can receive multiple health and/ or social services at one site."[16] This coordination usually occurs through Head Start programs. Since the MCHBG targets health services to pregnant women and children and promotes service coordination, it is a good candidate for collaboration with programs specializing in early childhood care.

- **Individuals with Disabilities Education Act (IDEA).** In addition to educational services for all children with special needs, IDEA provides for statewide early intervention systems and preschool services for young children with special needs from birth through age five. **Part H** requires participating states to plan, develop and implement a coordinated interagency system of early intervention services for eligible infants and toddlers. Special need, rather than family income, determines program eligibility. Participating states are required to provide case management services to infants and toddlers at no cost to the family. Additional services, such as follow-up medical care and treatment, must be coordinated with other funding sources, such as Medicaid, state appropriations, Maternal and Child Health Block Grants, Chapter 1 of the Elementary and Secondary Education Act of 1965, Part B of IDEA, or third-party payments.[17] Under Part H, Medicaid covers services to certain eligible infants and toddlers with disabilities.[18]

Part B requires public schools to serve eligible children with disabilities ages three to five. Services may be provided in community settings, such as early childhood programs. Medicaid reimburses for health-related services delivered to children with disabilities through early childhood programs or in other settings. Lawmakers should consider both Part H and Part B programs for coordination with other early care and education programs at the state level.

Early childhood programs provide a natural setting for health care agencies to connect with young children. Either health care agencies can come to the programs to provide services, such as health screenings or immunizations, or the programs can tap into federal funding sources for direct service reimbursement. Early childhood service programs are in a good position to collaborate with health programs because providers have a credible, ongoing relationship with families and can educate parents about good health and routinely

---

COORDINATING WITH MEDICAL HEALTH SERVICES

Early childhood programs can coordinate with Medicaid health services by

- providing information and processing applications as part of EPSDT's statutory mandate to conduct outreach to eligible populations.

- providing EPSDT services on site or referring children to other providers. Services can include immunizations, health screening and assessments, obtaining comprehensive health care histories and providing health education.

- providing Medicaid services to eligible children, pregnant women or family members. Such services can include family counseling, transportation to and from medical appointments or screening for child developmental delay.

- providing day care to infants and children with medically complex special needs.

—Zero To Three, National Center for Clinical Infant Programs
Medicaid and Child Care: Good Partnership Potential

monitor child health and development, provided workers are properly trained to do so.

State Activities: Coordinating Early Care and Health Services

A number of jurisdictions have taken action to promote child development and good health care in cooperation with early childhood programs. Examples provided in this chapter include state legislative activity or interagency agreements at the state and local levels. The latter examples, though not statutorily authorized, are good illustrations of an evolving area of collaboration and coordination that can help inform state policy development in the future.

For their part, state legislatures can address coordination through policies such as

- mandating linkages between state Medicaid and early childhood care and education programs;

- forging partnerships between health and child care services as part of broader system reform;

- including health components among requirements for state-funded early childhood and child care programs; and

GETTING FAMILIES TO MEDICAID

The Center for Budget and Policy Priorities' national outreach project works with early childhood programs to help eligible families enroll in Medicaid. Activities include helping Medicaid-eligible families fill out Medicaid application forms or referring them to Medicaid offices. In some states, such as **Maryland, Michigan** and **Missouri,** child care resource and referral agencies perform this outreach function. **Louisiana** reimburses Head Start programs for assisting families with their Medicaid applications. **Georgia** requires an EPSDT screening for children participating in the state preschool program, specifically targeting children who are eligible for Medicaid, but not enrolled in it.

- requiring early care providers to facilitate provision of certain health-related services.

To date, the bulk of state legislative activity has focused on the last option, particularly requiring providers to offer immunizations.

Links With Medicaid

According to the Children's Defense Fund, some state Medicaid agencies are taking the lead in efforts to involve early care providers in meeting their clients' health needs. The Children's Defense Fund reported in 1991 that Medicaid agencies in 10 states, the **District of Columbia** and **Puerto Rico** informed early childhood providers of EPSDT benefits. These states are **Alabama, Arizona, California, Colorado, Florida, New Mexico, Oregon, South Carolina, Washington** and **West Virginia.** In addition, two states, **California** and **Colorado,** actually certified day care providers as EPSDT screeners, and five states, **Alabama, California, Colorado, Mississippi** and **Nebraska,** certified Head Start programs.[19]

More recently, state agencies in **Arkansas** crafted agreements to provide health services to all children enrolled in the state's preschool program, Arkansas Better Chance (ABC). After ABC was created by the Legislature in 1991, grantees were required to provide EPSDT screenings to Medicaid-eligible children. Moreover, the state early childhood commission that oversees most state child care programs awarded a grant to the state health department to conduct health screenings for children not eligible for Medicaid who are enrolled in the ABC program. Because nearly one-quarter of ABC children are not eligible for Medicaid, this interagency grant agreement

enables the program to deliver comprehensive health screening services to all program participants. This action exemplifies an integrated child development strategy where linkages are established between health care, human services and education.[20]

In **Louisiana**, fully half of the state's school boards are enrolled as Medicaid screening providers, including most elementary, middle and high schools.[21] Schools are an effective hub for Medicaid outreach and service delivery for fiscal purposes, as well as for service delivery and integration. When federal funding is properly applied to achieve program goals, schools provide a rich source of required program matching funds without the allocation of additional state general revenues.[22] One parish (county) has expanded its screening program in all schools and hired more school nurses, financed through Medicaid.[23]

Coordination as Part of Comprehensive Reform

Indiana's approach exemplifies an effort to link health, social services and early childhood care and education programs by creating a policy framework for more comprehensive reform of state service systems for young children. The 1991 General Assembly created the Step Ahead Comprehensive Early Childhood Grant Program to provide financial assistance and incentives to coordinate services for families and children within or among counties. Programs eligible for grants under Step Ahead specialize in child care, preschool, parent information, school-age child care, early identification and intervention, maternal and child health and health and screening.

Some of the multifaceted goals of Step Ahead outlined in the legislation are:

- identification of and coordination among county programs;

- reduction in the incidence of developmental delay in preschool age children and in the associated costs of K-12 special education; and

- integration of children with disabilities into mainstream programs.

The legislative vision proposes that by the year 2000, all **Indiana** kindergartners will have "benefited since birth" from Step Ahead.

The legislation clearly requires coordination by Step Ahead grantees. Prospective grantees must demonstrate how certain county programs will be offered and coordinated. These programs include preschools, Head Start, child care, EPSDT, early intervention, parent information, school age child care, JOBS and programs specializing in children of teen parents, health, nutrition and immunization. More specifically, Step Ahead programs must cooperate with public schools, county health departments, WIC and programs for infants and toddlers with disabilities.[24] Around $1 million per year in state funds has gone to 18 county Step Ahead preschool pilot programs over the past few years, serving more than 2,200 children in 1995-96. Health services provided by some of these programs are hearing, speech and vision screening; home visits; parent education and support services; and immunizations. Last year, program administrators accessed other funds for the programs, such as school system funding, county option taxes, federal and state funds for teen parent programs, and Head Start and child care wraparound funds.[25]

In **North Carolina**, the legislatively authorized Smart Start Program also addresses health and early care linkages as part of more extensive reform. At least one Smart Start county delivers services to day care facilities from a mobile health unit. Such a unit accomplishes program outreach and coordination and solves transportation problems experienced by many low-income families. Smart Start, a major state gubernatorial and legislative reform initiative, is discussed in more detail in chapter 8, "Early Care and Family Support."

Health Requirements in State-Funded Preschools

Some state legislatures have linked health and early care needs by including health requirements in state-funded preschool programs. The most obvious example of this approach can be found in states like **Ohio** and **Oregon** where state program requirements resemble those of Head Start, including a comprehensive health component. A similar effort can be found in 13 states

and the District of Columbia that supplement Head Start allocations with state funds. More information about these states can be found in chapters 2 and 3.

The federal Head Start Bureau is also promoting better collaboration. It oversees five-year grants to 48 states, the District of Columbia and Puerto Rico to encourage collaboration between Head Start and other agencies, such as health departments. Even though virtually all Head Start children are eligible for Medicaid, only 70 percent are served by Medicaid's EPSDT program. As a result, coordination to increase usage is one of the goals of the New Jersey Head Start Collaboration Project.[26] Another state, **Alaska**, is working to improve dental health services to Head Start children.[27]

Required Health Services

In addition to promoting state linkages among Head Start, Medicaid and early care providers and broad reform initiatives that incorporate early care and health issues, state legislatures are also increasingly addressing specific health issues. Chief among these options are efforts to ensure that children in early childhood programs are immunized.

As of 1994, only 67 percent of all 2-year-olds were appropriately immunized. No more than 59 percent of 2-year-olds living below the poverty line and 71 percent of those above it were properly immunized.[28] Recognizing that immunization may be the most cost-effective public health tool available, some state legislatures have identified coordination with child care and early childhood education programs as a sensible option for increasing access to immunizations and preventing the spread of infectious diseases.[29]

At least 13 state laws passed between 1991 and 1995 require certain early care providers to ensure that enrolled children are immunized.[30] In 1993, **Kansas**

PAYING FOR IMMUNIZATIONS

The Federal Vaccines for Children Program provides free pediatric vaccines for all uninsured, Medicaid-eligible and Native American children. The law also covers insured children whose coverage does not include immunizations, if they obtain vaccines in federally qualified health centers or rural health centers. Early childhood programs are logical places for delivery of immunizations to eligible children under this new federal program.

required proof of immunization for children enrolling in school-operated preschool or child care programs, allowing for religious exemptions.[31] **South Carolina** also mandated certain immunization requirements for school-based programs.[32] In 1992, the **California** legislature established a child immunization outreach program. The legislation targets schools and community-based agencies among others and requires immunization for children under age 4 1/2 before admission to a family day care home.[33] Recent **Minnesota** law promotes the exchange of child immunization records between child care centers and health departments.[34]

Conclusion

The Carnegie Corporation's Task Force on Meeting the Needs of Young Children reports, "We can now say, with greater confidence than ever before, that the quality of young children's environment and social experience has a decisive, long-lasting impact on their well-being and ability to learn."[35] Adequate health care is a critical determinant of a child's development. Further, scientific evidence increasingly emphasizes the implications of the early years for other areas of public policy including crime and delinquency, school success, self-sufficiency and social adjustment. By recognizing the benefits of coordinating child health services with early childhood services, states are beginning to take advantage of an important strategy to address the health care needs of the nation's children. This collaboration can bring significant benefits in the future for both individual children and the nation's economy.

CHAPTER 6

CHILD CARE REGULATIONS AND QUALITY OF CARE

Introduction

The quality of early childhood programs is discussed repeatedly in the early childhood literature as the critical determinant of positive outcomes for children. Quality early childhood programs promote healthy child development by providing attentive and appropriate care in a safe and hygienic setting. The intent of government program regulation is to assure safe environments and to facilitate a nurturing relationship between child and caregiver. Regulation of early childhood programs is historically a state prerogative, and state legislatures play a pivotal role.

This chapter addresses state legislatures' policies with regard to regulation of child care settings to assure secure, quality environments. Regulation is cross-jurisdictional because it affects children's health, safety, care and education in out-of-home settings. Since legislative regulatory jurisdictions vary from state to state, discussion of child care regulations could reasonably be included in several chapters. For simplicity, it is presented in a separate chapter.

The Relationship Between Program Regulation and Quality

The linkage between quality care and regulation is not always evident to parents who are generally searching for a provider who will treat their child with the special attention that they themselves would give. Parents, and many legislators, believe that caregivers—not regulations—determine the quality of care. To be sure, the quality of the caregiver/child relationship is usually the most important factor for children. But appropriate regulation, consistently applied, can facilitate positive relationships. "For example, a program that assigns a small number of children to each staff member goes far toward achieving individualized attention for every child," notes the Carnegie Task Force on Meeting the Needs of Young Children.[1]

"Quality child care enables a young child to become emotionally secure, socially competent, and intellectually capable. . . .A quality program also attends to the basic issues of health and safety and emphasizes a partnership between parents and caregivers. Children who receive inadequate or barely adequate care are more likely later to feel insecure with teachers, to distrust other children, and to face possible later rejection by other children. Rejection by other children appears to be a powerful predictor of unhappy results, including early dropping out of school and delinquency."

—Carnegie Corporation of New York,
Starting Points: Meeting the Needs of Our Youngest Children

Furthermore, since relationships are key, a highly skilled, trained and professional group of caregivers is important, as is a framework of reasonable regulatory standards to hold the profession accountable.

Although legislators must balance issues related to over regulation, which can have unintended, detrimental consequences for the availability and cost of care, perhaps more pressing policy considerations concern the disparity between current state regulatory environments and the research findings on determinants of quality care. According to the research, characteristics that determine program quality are:

1. staff qualifications and training;

2. staff/child ratios;

3. child development curriculum;

4. group size;

5. provisions for health, safety and nutrition;

6. appropriate evaluation procedures; and

7. parental involvement.[2]

Collectively, these characteristics contribute to overall program quality.

THE RELATIONSHIP BETWEEN CAREGIVER AND CHILD

"The single most important factor in quality care is the relationship between the child and the caregiver. Children who receive warm and sensitive caregiving are more likely to trust caregivers, to enter school ready and eager to learn, and to get along well with other children. The quality of caregiver-child relations depends in part on the sensitivity of the caregiver and in part on the ratio of caregivers to children, the number of children in a group, and the education and training levels of the caregiver."

—Carnegie Corporation of New York, *Starting Points*

The Importance of High-Quality Care

Consider the following selected findings reported in the early care literature:

- A 1992 study by Deborah Phillips found that "centers in states with more stringent child care regulations offer higher quality care, on average, than do centers in states with more lax regulations."[3]

- Children who suffer poor quality in teaching relationships do not do as well on tests for social development and language development. Indicators of lower program quality are lower staff salaries, fewer benefits and poorer working conditions, all factors that contribute to inadequate teaching relationships with children.[4]

- In a study commissioned by the **California** General Assembly on changing child/staff ratios, researchers found that when a teacher was responsible for too many children, "children were observed to be more uninvolved in classroom activities."[5]

- The 1995 study *Cost, Quality and Child Outcomes in Child Care Centers* found that quality of child care is primarily related to higher staff-to-child ratios, staff education, and administrators' experience.[6]

- The National Child Care Staffing Study documented disturbing results for children's social and language development when they were enrolled in programs with high staff turnover. Children in centers with higher turnover rates spent less time engaged in social activities with peers and more time in aimless wandering.[7]

- According to the National Day Care Study, "the children in smaller groups made the greatest gains in standardized tests of learning and vocabulary."[8]

- Children with teachers who engage in more appropriate caregiving have been found to have higher scores on tests of language and cognition. Moreover, factors that influence whether teachers engage in appropriate caregiving include child-to-staff ratios, group sizes, curriculum, teacher training and teachers' level of formal education.[9]

- The quality of developmental activities in programs examined as part of the National Child Care Staffing Study were found to be inadequate in almost one-third of the classrooms in child care centers and one-half of those serving infants.[10]

- A 1994 study conducted by the Families and Work Institute found the quality of care in family child care and other home-based settings to be extremely inadequate based on a variety of measures ranging from space and furnishings to learning activities. This is particularly disturbing since common perceptions are that family child care offers a more individualized and home-like atmosphere.[11]

But research does not consistently correlate quality with any particular type of program. Instead, factors like staff wages and reasonable numbers of children per

---

COST, QUALITY AND CHILD CARE OUTCOMES

A 1995 study of 401 centers concluded that states with less stringent standards had a greater number of low-quality centers and that quality in the classroom is directly associated with higher staff-to-child ratios. The study also found that higher quality costs more, but not a great deal more. On average, the better quality services in the study cost 10 percent more than centers providing typical care. This suggests that relatively modest investments—wisely spent—can reap significant benefits in improving the quality of child care services. The study also reaffirmed other research findings that centers with higher staff wages were of better quality and that most centers offered services well below professional standards. The research suggests that for children—across a variety of family backgrounds—good center care enhances their development and poor care impairs it. Nonetheless parents in the study tended to overestimate the quality of care in programs attended by their children.

—Cost, Quality and Outcomes Project, University of Colorado at Denver
Cost, Quality and Outcomes in Child Care Centers

---

teacher have been associated with quality in the research. As continuing research on the components of quality care becomes available, state legislators are translating the information into state regulatory processes.

The following sections address the role of regulation in promoting healthy child development. Specific areas of discussion are (1) the regulatory environment, vis à vis the role of state legislatures; (2) the scope of regulation in early childhood programs; (3) initiatives related to staffing and quality; and (4) enforcement. Each section includes state examples.

State Regulatory Environment

With the exception of Head Start, regulation of early care and education programs is primarily a prerogative of state and local government. Consequently, program regulation varies from state to state. States assure safe settings and quality programming by regulating all types of early childhood programs: child care centers, family day care homes, preschools and school-age programs. With some notable exceptions, state regulation applies to both publicly and privately operated programs. Different types of programs, however, frequently are authorized and regulated by separate state agencies. This can result in similar programs operating under separate jurisdictions subject to entirely different sets of standards.[12] Public preschools, for example, are often regulated by education agencies whereas private child care programs may be regulated by social services or health departments. Programs that receive multiple funds may be regulated by several different systems.

Unless otherwise noted, this chapter focuses primarily on regulation of state child care programs—not Head Start or state prekindergarten programs. Head Start programs operate under federal regulations. Preschool programs may be regulated by a separate credentialing system for public schools; however, only an estimated 8 percent of preschools are actually operated by the schools.[13] A full discussion of the three separate regulatory structures is beyond the scope of this publication. Therefore, this chapter focuses on the primary regulatory system to date, child care programs. Legislators interested in cross-jurisdictional early care and education approaches, however, will need to thoughtfully consider regulatory policies and practices that cross systems.

Reflecting the variety of program operators and types, the extent of state regulation varies. Licensing, which involves government inspection, is the most comprehensive form of state regulation. Lesser degrees of regulation include registration with the state or self-certification that programs meet certain requirements. In some states family child care homes are required only to register with the state. In cases where family child care homes are licensed, requirements are generally less stringent than for child care centers. Moreover, some types of programs, such as those operated by public recreation departments, family day care providers or religious groups, may be exempt from licensing and other forms of regulation altogether.

Though states' regulatory frameworks are often statutory, most legislatures delegate specific, detailed rule making to a state agency. The **Idaho** Legislature, however, retains sole authority over rule making; hence, regulatory requirements for early childhood facilities are developed in, and subject to, the normal legislative process.[14] More commonly, the process begins when the legislature determines which programs are subject to state licensing and designates a state agency to issue and enforce specific requirements. Rules are usually developed through the state's existing administrative rules process, which generally requires extensive review by affected parties, including, in this case, input from parents and other members of the early childhood community. Since licensing includes provisions for sanitation, health and fire safety, enforcement of these standards is often coordinated with agencies responsible for monitoring such state and local requirements.

The legislature maintains oversight of the licensing process by reviewing administrative rules, funding enforcement personnel and by detailing important requirements in statute. To date, 41 state legislatures review administrative rules for compliance with both statutory authority and legislative intent.[15] It is usually more difficult to change a statute than an administrative rule. Consequently, legislatures incorporate certain requirements in statute. This statutory base assures the "staying power" of certain basic requirements.

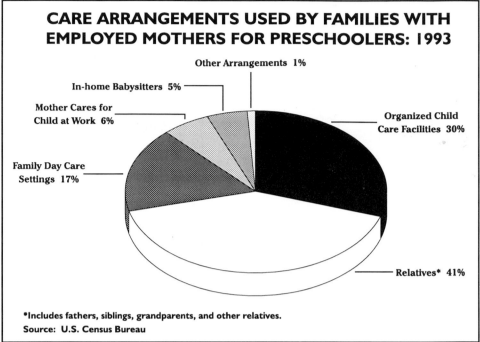

CARE ARRANGEMENTS USED BY FAMILIES WITH EMPLOYED MOTHERS FOR PRESCHOOLERS: 1993

Other Arrangements 1%
In-home Babysitters 5%
Mother Cares for Child at Work 6%
Organized Child Care Facilities 30%
Family Day Care Settings 17%
Relatives* 41%

*Includes fathers, siblings, grandparents, and other relatives.
Source: U.S. Census Bureau

REGULATED HOME CARE IS BETTER

A recent study of 226 regulated and unregulated home and relative caregivers in Dallas, Los Angeles and Charlotte, N.C., rated only 9 percent of the child care provided by relatives or other home-based caregivers as good quality and 35 percent as inadequate. The other 56 percent were rated as adequate/custodial. The study points to lack of regulation as one reason for poor-quality programs. Of the 166 family child care homes studied, around two-thirds (112) were regulated and about one third (54) were unregulated. (Eighty-one percent of the unregulated family child care homes were illegally unregulated.) Virtually all of the 60 relative providers studied were exempt from regulation.

Using six areas of caregiving practice as a global measurement of quality, the study found that "regulated providers are rated as more sensitive and observed to be offering more responsive care than nonregulated or relative caregivers." Of the regulated homes studied, only 13 percent were rated as inadequate, while half of the nonregulated homes were rated as inadequate and 69 percent of relative care were rated as inadequate. The study also found that regulated family child care providers are more likely to plan activities for children, receive relevant training and be committed to their jobs than nonregulated or relative caregivers. Even in many regulated homes, however, quality was lacking; only 12 percent received a good quality rating. Only 3 percent of nonregulated homes were rated as good quality.

—Families and Work Institute
The Study of Children in Family Child Care and Relative Care

Scope of Regulation in Early Childhood Programs

Although most state regulatory frameworks represent minimal standards, "requirements for family day care homes average 16.6 pages; those for group day care centers, 30.2 pages."[16] A significant number of providers are exempt from standards in some states. As recently as 1990, the Children's Defense Fund reported that 43 percent of all children in out-of-home child care were unprotected by state regulation largely because certain care settings are exempt from coverage—even for minimal health and safety standards.[17]

Family day care homes, for example, are typically exempt from regulation, or are subject to less stringent rules. This exemption concerns policymakers because large numbers of children are cared for in such settings. To address disparities in regulation, some legislatures are extending coverage to programs that have previously been either totally unregulated or excluded from specific regulations.

State Activities

In 1993, the **Virginia** Legislature extended regulation and state inspection to religious-based programs. The law imposes licensing requirements on additional family day care homes and extends voluntary registration requirements to exempt homes.[18] **Nevada** extended statutory regulations in 1993 to encompass arrangements in which at least one child is receiving care for compensation.[19] In 1991, the **Maryland** Legislature adopted a unique approach that establishes a 14-month amnesty period for unregistered family day care homes to meet state requirements while remaining in operation.[20] **Maryland** created the Family Day Care Provider Direct Grant Fund to reimburse providers up to $500 for expenses incurred in meeting state and local regulations. Grantees must agree to provide at least one year of care for a subsidized child, an infant, a child with special needs or a school-age child.[21] The state also has a loan fund of between $1,000 and $5,000 to assist child care facilities in meeting regulatory requirements.[22] The **Ohio** General Assembly required licensure for preschool programs with standards meeting or exceeding those applied to child care programs.[23] **New York** legislators created a mandatory registration system for family day care homes caring for

three to six children and for school-age child care programs.[24] In 1989, the **Tennessee** legislature required child care centers operated by certain church-related schools to be regulated by the Department of Education.[25]

State Initiatives Related to Quality and Staffing

To date, most state child care regulations address "minimal...criteria for (the) legal operation of child care facilities and do not necessarily reflect high-quality standards."[26] As state lawmakers learn more about the relationship between quality and state standards, however, more legislatures are addressing staffing levels, training and qualifications, compensation and screening in an effort to improve program quality. State illustrations in these areas follow.

Child-to-Staff Ratios

Quality child care can be provided only if the caregiver is not responsible for too many children. The National Association for the Education of Young Children recommends certain staffing levels dependent on the number of children and their ages to ensure that providers can offer children the appropriate level of attention.

State legislatures have been attempting to meet or exceed those standards to ensure safe, nurturing child care. **North Carolina**'s standard for staff-to-infant ratios was below recommended levels when the issue came before the Legislative Research Commission during a child care study in 1992-93. Resulting legislation lowered staff-to-infant ratios from 1:7 to 1:5. In garnering support, legislative sponsors successfully convinced colleagues that protection of young children's health and safety was worth the two-year $3.6 million price tag to upgrade staffing for public child care programs.[27] Six years ago, the **Florida** Legislature also improved child staff ratios for prekindergarten programs and child care centers.[28]

Staff Training

State regulations related to staff training are designed to improve competency and knowledge of the best practices by early care workers. Most often, these regulations take the form of specifying minimum education qualifications or requiring preservice and ongoing staff training. Administrative regulations and statutory requirements for staff training vary from state to state and by program type. For example, 34 states require training for regulated family child care operators.[29] But the state requirements range from two hours every five years in **Iowa** to 20 hours per year in **Texas**.[30] In contrast, a significant number of states require training for child care center staff. Forty-nine states, the **District of Columbia, Puerto Rico** and the **Virgin Islands** require preservice training or experience, or both, and 47 states require on-the-job training.[31]

Several state legislatures have recently upgraded training requirements for child care and early childhood education providers. Between 1991 and 1996 at least 20 state legislatures passed laws to strengthen training requirements.[32] State laws focus on preservice or ongoing training. For example, **Kentucky** law requires newly hired staff to complete six training hours within the first three months of employment. Training must cover basic health, safety and sanitation; recognizing and reporting child abuse; and developmentally appropriate child care.[33] **Idaho** law requires child care center employees to receive a minimum of four hours training annually.[34] Other laws specifically recognize the health impact of early childhood workers' training. **California**, for instance, enacted a law in 1992 requiring centers and licensed family day care providers to have at least 15 hours of training in preventive health practices.[35]

State lawmakers are also addressing child care training by targeting use of state-administered school loan programs. The **California** Legislature established the Child Development Teacher Loan Assumption Program to provide loans for students who agree to work in child care and development.[36] In **Maryland**'s child care tuition assistance program, approved in 1990, early childhood students are eligible for loans of no more than $2,000 annually for up to four years. After graduation, loan repayments are waived for each year of work in child care. The **Maryland** General Assembly approved $100,000 for this program.[37] **Virginia**'s legislature recently extended the Virginia Teaching Scholarship Loan Program to child care teachers. A student can receive an annual loan of $2,000, with a year of the loan forgiven for each year of teaching.[38] **Pennsylvania** enacted legislation in 1993 to provide a loan

forgiveness award of $2,500 per year, capped at $10,000, to child care workers. To qualify for a forgiveness award, an individual must work in an approved child care facility and earn either a bachelor's or an associate degree.[39]

Staff Wages

If appropriate training, education and low staff-to-child ratios are important in achieving program quality and positive outcomes for children, it follows that early childhood programs must be able to attract qualified staff. The National Child Care Staffing Study contends that the most important predictor of quality care for children is staff wages.[40] In order to attract and maintain competent workers, early childhood programs must compensate staff adequately. But workers in the field are notoriously underpaid. In fact, real wages for the lowest paid child care assistant teachers actually fell 1.5 percent between 1988 and 1992 to $8,890 per year, teachers themselves averaged around $15,500 per year.[41] Low pay results in a high staff turnover rate. This dynamic contributes to disruptions in the continuity of care for many young children, which is the opposite of what children need. For the increasing number of infants and toddlers in child care, stability is particularly crucial.

CONTINUITY OF CARE IS ESSENTIAL

The care of children is changing. More children are moving into child care, at younger ages, and for longer periods of time. What they need is a special kind of care. It's not babysitting, and it's not school. It is a continuing relationship with a few caring people in an intimate setting. Just as they need parents who read and respond to them with ease and who give them the sense of being important, so infants need this from one or two particular child care providers. And continuity of care is essential. When infants lose a caregiver, they really lose a sense of themselves and of the way things work.

—Zero To Three
Heart Start: The Emotional Foundations of School Readiness

Some state approaches focus on making the occupation attractive by increasing wages or developing provider incentives for competency-based pay. For example in 1990, **Maine, Massachusetts, New York** and **Pennsylvania** established salary enhancement grant programs for child care workers with appropriations ranging from $12 million in New York to $800,000 in

LOW PAY FOR IMPORTANT WORK

The National Center for the Early Childhood Work Force (NCECW) sponsors "National Worthy Wage Day" every April to raise awareness on compensation issues. Former NCECW Executive Director Marcy Whitebook argues that low pay for early childhood workers is partially due to inherently lower pay scales for women and people of color. According to a recent NCECW survey, 98 percent of child care workers in four major U.S. cities are women, and a third are women of color. Moreover, "child care is something families have not traditionally paid for. We don't think of it as skilled work that we want to pay for," says Whitebook. The Worthy Wage Coalition is calling for a minimum average wage of $10 an hour and comprehensive health care benefits. This level would bring child care workers wages in line with national averages.[44]

Maine.[42] In 1993, **North Carolina** appropriated $1 million per year for the TEACH (Training, Education and Compensation Helps) program that increases salaries for child care workers who receive more training and education.[43] 1993 **Maine** legislation authorizes differential reimbursement rates for programs meeting higher standards.[45] **Ohio, Vermont** and **Wisconsin** also authorize such variable reimbursements. In 1996, **Florida** enacted a higher reimbursement rate for regulated providers in an effort to encourage better quality providers.[46] Generally, state legislative reimbursement authority extends only to a segment of the child care market—programs that accept publicly subsidized children. Thus, equitable distribution of wage supplements or provider incentives is difficult.

Staff Screening

Recent legislative activity has focused on screening staff for records of child abuse or crime. Protecting children in early childhood programs from child abuse, sexual abuse, exploitation and abduction are major health and safety concerns. Screening early childhood personnel is one approach state legislatures have taken to prevent children from being placed in harmful early childhood settings.

Statutory requirements for screening employees vary from state to state. As of July 1995, 47 states required criminal history checks for employees in licensed child care

centers or regulated family child care homes.[47] In addition, many states include checking the state child abuse registry as part of the screening process.[48] In general, a registry is a listing of abuse and neglect cases handled by a child protection agency, which may or may not have resulted in criminal prosecution and conviction. In contrast, a criminal records check assesses past criminal convictions, which include crimes against children. Some states require a federal criminal history check through the Federal Bureau of Investigation in addition to searching state records.

Opponents express two primary concerns about criminal history checks: (1) the costs are more than for central registry checks and can burden employees or agencies and (2) the time it takes to process criminal history checks delays hiring. Costs and turnaround time for state criminal history checks range from $5 and five to seven days in **Virginia** and $17 and three days in **Colorado** to $27 and 45 to 90 days in **California.** Moreover, it costs an extra $23 to process a federal FBI check.

In 1993, the **New Jersey** Legislature replaced criminal history background checks of family day care providers with a central registry search when it found that costs associated with the background checks were decreasing family day care home registrations.[49] The situation illustrates that well-meaning policies sometime have unintended consequences. In addition, it is the continuing responsibility of state legislatures to find a balance between protecting children and limiting the burdens placed on early childhood providers. It is also

SECONDHAND SMOKE IN CHILD CARE SETTINGS

In 1996, 33 states prohibited smoking in child care centers, 12 states restricted smoking, and 8 states had no restrictions. In 1996 35 states prohibited smoking in family child care homes, 8 restricted smoking, and 13 states had no restrictions. (Five states were counted twice because they prohibited smoking in larger family child care homes, but only placed restrictions in smaller homes).[50]

important to note that child abuse registries can contain records of minor incidents that were substantiated but do not constitute a real threat to child safety.

The **California** Legislature has taken an innovative approach to screen providers who are legally exempt from regulation. It created the "Trustline" system in 1991 to list and provide information on all license-exempt providers, such as nannies and babysitters. Parents can use the Trustline to check unlicensed caregivers for certain criminal convictions and a history of child abuse. Parents must pay a one-time fee of $85 to use the Trustline system.[51] **Virginia** state law extends criminal history check requirements to religious providers exempt from licensure.[52] In 1994, **Iowa** enacted authorization for resource and referral agencies to access the child abuse registry regarding all providers who wish to receive referrals. The law applies to both regulated and unregulated providers and the state absorbs the costs.[53]

Enforcement

Child care regulations and standards are meaningful only if they are enforced. The U.S. General Accounting Office (GAO) and the U.S. Department of Health and Human Services' Office of the Inspector General conducted surveys of states to determine their effectiveness in enforcement. Both found that the states are having trouble "protecting children from care that does not meet minimum safety and health standards." In fact, the GAO report notes that "staffing and budget cuts in several states have reduced on-site monitoring, a key oversight activity that is necessary for the enforcement of standards."[54] Moreover, the Children's Defense Fund reported in 1994 that half the states do not require inspections of providers who care for small numbers of children.[55]

According to the GAO, two-thirds of state licensing directors ranked on-site monitoring as the most effective way to ensure compliance.[56] Yet 18 states have reduced the frequency of on-site visits since 1989, and 13 states were unable to meet their own monitoring requirements for centers, largely due to state budget problems. Twenty states did not meet the National Association for the Education of Young Children's (NAEYC) standard for states to conduct at least one unannounced visit to each center every year. NAEYC actually recommends two visits per year, at least one unannounced. Thirty-nine states did not

meet the latter standard when the survey was conducted in 1992.[57] Furthermore, the Office of the Inspector General concluded that health and safety problems in child care and early childhood education in Native American facilities in **Delaware, North Carolina, South Carolina** and **Wisconsin** were because of either insufficient inspections or their prior announcement.[58] Over the past few years, legislators in **California, Kentucky, Montana** and **West Virginia** have enacted laws to increase or improve unannounced inspections.

Next to on-site visits, the GAO reported that 14 state licensing directors ranked imposing sanctions the second most effective tool for centers in ensuring compliance with standards and regulations.[59] Sanctions include imposing a corrective plan, fines or closing the facility. In 1990, the **Florida** Legislature enacted a law allowing for a fine up to $500 per day for violations of child care standards that could cause or have caused death or serious harm to a child.[60] In 1993, legislation was adopted in **Texas** to require a license to be suspended, a facility to be closed and children to be placed elsewhere for standard violations that create a threat to the health and safety of the children.[61] By 1993, 41 states had used the Child Care and Development Block Grant to fund general state child care licensing and monitoring efforts.[62]

Conclusion

A number of professional organizations recommend standards for all types of early childhood programs. The most well-known is the National Association for the Education of Young Children (NAEYC), whose standards address staff-child interaction, curriculum, staff-parent interaction, staff qualifications and development, compensation and administration, staff/child ratios and group sizes, physical environment, health and safety, nutrition and evaluation.[63] In addition, NAEYC has an accreditation program for centers based on their recommended standards. Some states including **Maine, Ohio,** and **Vermont** have legislatively tied child care reimbursement to professional standards.[64] In **Maine,** for example, higher reimbursement rates are available for providers who meet NAEYC accreditation standards.

Chapter 7

EARLY CHILDHOOD SERVICES AND WELFARE REFORM

Introduction

In August 1996, President Clinton and Congress enacted the most significant piece of social welfare legislation in the past half century. The Personal Responsibility and Work Opportunity Reconciliation Act (P.L. 104-193) abolished Aid to Families with Dependent Children (AFDC), Job Opportunity and Basic Skills (JOBS), and Emergency Assistance programs and replaced them with Temporary Assistance for Needy Families (TANF). P.L. 104-193 ends the federal guarantee of cash assistance for the nation's poor families and children begun during the New Deal. Instead the new legislation allows time-limited federal assistance to individuals through block grants to the states.

At the same time, the legislation ends the federal entitlement to child care established under the 1988 Family Support Act for working welfare recipients, those in work and training programs, and—for 12 months—those who leave welfare for work. Congress opted for a new six-year block grant to the states for child care services for TANF participants. The legislation consolidates four federal child care funding streams, allocates more money than was expected under the previous system, and requires the program to be administered by the state agency responsible for the Child Care and Development Block Grant of 1990 (CCDBG).

Under the welfare legislation, the lifetime limit on assistance—including cash or other services provided with federal TANF funds—is set at five years, and individuals are required to work in exchange for assistance after two years. In addition, states must meet stringent new work participation requirements that must include 50 percent of a state's adult TANF population within six years, or the state will lose part of its block grant. These new work obligations are expected to increase the demand for child care in the states dramatically.

States have considerable flexibility in fashioning child care programs to meet new demands, but—in the long term—they will have fewer federal resources available to them than under the old system. States initially receive more money under the new block grant than they did before. But as work requirements and the demand for child care increases, the federal share under the block grant will remain the same instead of increasing with the need, as it did in an open-ended entitlement.

Despite the new law's limitations, the integration of federal funding streams offers a significant opportunity for states to streamline and consolidate child care services under one administrative structure. It removes federal

barriers to more efficient administration of child care funding streams, which in the past had separate rules and regulations. Their integration under the CCDBG paves the way for state consolidation and potential administrative savings. And the demands precipitated by the law create new incentives to better coordinate welfare-related child care programs with state preschool and Head Start services to maximize resources for the influx of welfare recipients with new work obligations.

State lawmakers are pivotal in the successful implementation of P.L. 104-193 because legislatures must appropriate the new funds and make a variety of related policy choices. Perhaps most important, state legislatures face critical new responsibilities in assuring that child care services are both available to maintain families' transition to the work force and good enough to promote school-readiness and healthy outcomes for children from welfare families.

> Quality child care programs can achieve a multitude of important social welfare goals. They can help parents not only to work, but also to be better parents. Quality programs can help stem child abuse and offer needed health, social services, or parenting education, while actually improving children's developmental progress, especially in terms of their school-readiness. A "two-generation" child care strategy thus considers both parents' and children's needs. It addresses work force development and child development as complementary—not competing—policy goals.

To carry out these new responsibilities, however, state policymakers can draw on a considerable body of experience. Even before passage of the new federal law, lawmakers across the country recognized the crucial role of child care in promoting both self-sufficiency and healthy child development. In recent years, legislatures pioneered the expansion of child care services as part of welfare reform and innovated new approaches to support quality. This chapter will present the rationale for linking child care and welfare reform policy goals under a two generation strategy, outline the provisions of TANF and the new child care block grant, and discuss their interrelationships, detail child care implementation issues under the new law, and provide examples of state legislative responses to similar policy questions.

Child Care and the Transition Off Welfare

The rationale for providing child care assistance under state welfare programs recognizes the crucial role of child care in promoting self-sufficiency. Too often, it is thought, women return to welfare because they cannot afford basics such as health insurance and child care in the entry-level, mostly minimum wage jobs that are available to workers with less education and experience. Recipients leaving welfare for jobs can find themselves less well-off than on welfare because of the high costs of these basics. In addition, difficulties in obtaining reliable child care have been found to affect recipients' ability to retain jobs or to successfully complete work and training programs.

Recent state experiences with welfare reform reinforce the notion that child care is integral to moving welfare families into the work force. The U.S. General Accounting Office (GAO) has found that child care subsidies make a decisive difference in whether poor mothers work: A 1994 GAO report indicates that a subsidy for the full cost of child care increases the probability of poor mothers working by 15 percentage points.[1] Evaluations of GAIN, **California**'s pioneering welfare and job training program, found that mothers who were worried about their children's safety and who did not trust their child care providers were twice as likely to drop out than mothers who were satisfied with their care arrangements.[2] A Minneapolis study found that nearly a quarter of low-income families waiting for child care subsidies quit their jobs or training and returned to welfare.[3]

A study of single parents in **Illinois** found that child care problems kept:

- 42 percent of recipients from working full time;
- 39 percent from looking for work as much as they wanted to;
- 26 percent from working as much as they desired; and
- 39 percent from going to school.

Difficulties with child care contributed to families' return to welfare in **Illinois**. In addition, 42 percent of teenage parents in the study quit school within the previous year—in part due to child care problems.[4] Similarly, a **Massachusetts** study found that one-third of mothers who left welfare for jobs returned after one year because of child care problems.[5] Furthermore, a 1996 GAO report indicates that single parents who receive child care assistance are more likely to complete training and obtain a job or enroll in school.[6]

Benefits to Parents

These findings indicate the importance of providing child care to welfare clients to allow parents to work or participate in education and training programs. Because those moving from welfare into the work force seldom obtain high-paying jobs, child care expenses alone can interfere with a successful transition.[7] For example, child care expenses for poor families consume 18 percent of their income, compared with 7 percent for families earning more than the federal poverty level.[8] Moreover, AFDC recipients are more likely to obtain entry-level jobs that do not offer benefits. This fact makes subsidies for child care and other benefits, such as health care, critical in efforts to "make work pay."

Benefits to Children

The availability of child care makes it possible for parents to work. But quality care—as opposed to custodial care—is critical to achieving the complementary, but longer-term, policy goal of breaking the cycle of poverty. As discussed throughout this book, quality child care programs give children in welfare families the essential tools they need to grow into productive adults. The complementary goals of child development and work force development require policymakers to consider the quality of child care programming provided to children in welfare families. Too often, these children are at risk of poor outcomes in school and in other areas. A 1995 study of 790 welfare families in Atlanta, for example, found that the preschool-age children, on average, scored low in tests of vocabulary and school readiness. Forty-two percent of the 3- and 4-year-olds answered correctly only half or fewer of the questions related to school readiness. Study authors challenge policymakers considering welfare policies to assure the quality of child care:

"The mothers in this study—as well as mothers in other welfare studies—indicated a preference for center-based child care. Such settings are an opportunity to improve children's school readiness if the quality of care is good. State officials could require that centers receiving public subsidies to care for children in welfare families meet certain standards of quality in child care."[9]

State investments in quality child care can improve

WELFARE AND SCHOOL-READINESS

"Seventeen percent of all preschool children in America—3.6 million children ages 0-6—recently resided in an AFDC household. AFDC households with preschool children score extremely high on a variety of risk factors associated with school unreadiness—single parenting, poverty, adolescent parenting, adult educational dropouts. If children living in AFDC households are at four times the risk of starting school unready to learn than other children, this means that nearly half the children who start school not ready to learn live in AFDC households. In the long term, it may be more important to society's economic well-being whether these children start school ready to learn than whether their heads-of-households—whose numbers represent less than 3.5 percent of the civilian labor force—secure employment."

Charles Bruner, Testimony to the Working Group on Welfare Reform, Nashville, Tennessee, 1993.

school readiness and other outcomes for children. This is particularly important because children from welfare families are nearly one-third more likely to suffer either from delays in growth and development, a significant emotional or behavioral problem, or a learning disability. Such children have a greater need for more comprehensive and higher-quality services than other children.[10]

Elements of quality programming include well-trained and adequately paid staff, fewer children for each provider, curriculum and activities appropriate to young children, parental involvement and other characteristics. Based on the same research on the High/Scope Perry Preschool project documented in earlier chapters, low-income preschoolers who enroll in high-quality early childhood programs are more likely to complete high school, get jobs, and be married at age 27 than their peers without experience in a high-quality program. These children are also less likely to be school dropouts, dependent on welfare, or repeatedly arrested.[11] Working with children of welfare clients offers an opportunity to target children most at risk and most likely to benefit from high-quality programs. Well-designed child care programs can offer the opportunity to meet two goals: economic self-sufficiency for families and healthy development of children.

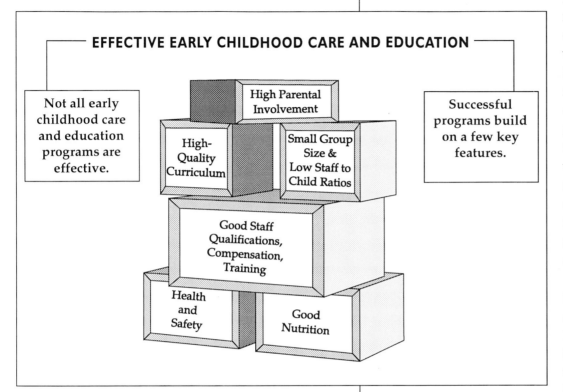

EFFECTIVE EARLY CHILDHOOD CARE AND EDUCATION

Not all early childhood care and education programs are effective.

High Parental Involvement

High-Quality Curriculum

Small Group Size & Low Staff to Child Ratios

Good Staff Qualifications, Compensation, Training

Health and Safety

Good Nutrition

Successful programs build on a few key features.

With the advent of federal welfare reform, state lawmakers face a daunting challenge in maintaining a "two-generation" child care strategy, one that meets the needs of children for quality—and sometimes enriched— programming to improve their long-term outcomes, while meeting parents' immediate needs for care that enables them to work. Although the additional work obligations mandated under the federal law create significant new pressures to build the supply of child care, a "two-generation" strategy challenges lawmakers to ensure that the expanded infrastructure is not just safe for children, but simultaneously prepares them for success in school and in life.

The States and Welfare Reform

The AFDC program was created in the 1930s to assist poor, widowed mothers in raising their children at a time when work opportunities for women were not only limited but culturally less acceptable. Today, the nature of welfare has changed. Caseloads now include large proportions of never-married women—many of whom first had children as teenagers. At the same time, most non-AFDC mothers now participate in the work force.

Historically, most single mothers have worked, even when their children were very young. Recently, however, married mothers also entered the work force in great numbers, so today they are as likely to be working as single mothers. This has changed public expectations about whether mothers with young children should work.[12]

Public attitudes toward welfare demand change. According to a 1995 public opinion poll, 93 percent of Americans want welfare reform. Six in ten (59 percent) thought the welfare system should be "fundamentally overhauled." Respondents' top concern about welfare was not its cost to taxpayers but its effects on recipients. Almost two-thirds of respondents complained that welfare "encourages people to adopt the wrong lifestyle and values." Furthermore, even welfare recipients disliked the system, nine in 10 recipients in the same survey also supported changes in welfare.

Over the past three decades, social welfare policy has begun to emphasize the concept of welfare as a "social contract," where recipients work, train, or study in exchange for benefits. This concept was a central theme of the reforms included in the Family Support Act of 1988. More recently, consensus has continued to grow that welfare should be work-based: those on welfare who are able to work should do so. Three-quarters of the 1995 survey respondents said that recipients should be required to enroll in job training and education. More

LESSONS FROM THE AFDC PROGRAM

Data about the AFDC program in the recent past provide important information as states implement new federal welfare reforms. In fiscal year 1995, 4.8 million U.S. families received AFDC at a cost of $16 billion in federal money accounting for 1 percent of the federal budget.[13] Seventy percent of the AFDC caseload was made up of families headed by a single or divorced parent, another 11 percent was headed by a parent separated from a spouse.[14] Sixty-five percent of the adult caseload is between age 20 and 34.[15]

Traditionally, AFDC served mostly women and children, but the profile of female recipients has changed over the years. Most recently, welfare moms are more likely to have never been married and are less likely to have child support orders.[16] According to a recent General Accounting Office (GAO) report, compared with those in 1976, female AFDC recipients in 1992 were more likely to have a high school diploma and have fewer children. However, they were also poorer than in the previous decade.[17]

Other characteristics of families receiving AFDC in 1995 include:

• The average family had 2.8 people;
• The average age of a child was 7 years, 5 months;
• Fifty-nine percent of families had a child under 6[18]

In 1995, AFDC work participation rates were set at 20 percent. And states could exempt families with children under 3 from JOBS, the AFDC work and training program. Some did so because of the high cost and scarcity of child care for infants and toddlers and to focus resources on those the research shows are most likely to succeed in the work force, that is, women with older children.[19] The AFDC child care guarantee meant that recipients could be required to participate in work or training only if needed child care was provided. In 1995, some 35 percent of required JOBS participants nationwide were exempted from work and training requirements because of child care problems. In fact, only 6.4 percent of all AFDC families received publicly subsidized child care in 1994, largely as a result of low JOBS participation.[20]

Researcher LaDonna Pavetti of the Urban Institute, who has examined the likely impact of federal time limits on recent welfare caseloads, reports that understanding how much time people spend on welfare requires examining two seemingly contradictory facts:

• Most families who ever use welfare do so for short periods (three years or less)
• About 70 percent of recipients at a given time have

received AFDC for more than two years and almost half (48 percent) have been on the rolls more than 5 years.

In looking at welfare populations in two different ways—the first including the larger group of families who ever seek welfare help and the other including the smaller group who are currently on the rolls—one gets different impressions about welfare usage. Pavetti's research indicates that the strongest predictors of whether a recipient leaves for employment are recent work experience and educational attainment. She warns that women who spend long periods of time on welfare—those most likely to reach the five-year time limit under TANF—are precisely those with the most limited job prospects. Pavetti's research on AFDC recipients indicates that half of those who spend more than five years on assistance entered AFDC with no labor market experience, and 63 percent have less than a high school education. She points out that these long-term families will need considerably more assistance than is usually provided under traditional welfare-to-work programs to make a successful transition.[21]

Welfare researchers Bane and Ellwood describe some long-term recipients as " 'cyclers': people who move on and off welfare, apparently trying to leave, but unable to do so permanently. They obtain a job or find additional support elsewhere, but the improvement is only temporary. Their child becomes ill or they miss a day of work, and they are back on welfare."[22] Pavetti's research suggests that a significant proportion of recipients return to welfare after short periods off the rolls. She found that 42 percent of new recipients had received AFDC benefits previously.[23] These data suggest some families need longer-term or periodic help in maintaining self-sufficiency.

Despite the concern about welfare usage, however, in 1994 only 63 percent of children living below the federal poverty level received AFDC.[24] The 1996 median AFDC payment of $377 per month, or $4,524 per year, for a family of three[25] — one adult and two children—is significantly lower than the official poverty index of $12,980 for a family of three.[26] In no states do welfare benefits and food stamps raise recipients to the poverty level. When adjusted for inflation, benefit levels have actually declined. Between 1975 and 1996, average AFDC benefits per family dropped 44.6 percent.[27] Furthermore, some families get welfare because their wages were low. In 1995, 11 percent of AFDC families had wage earnings low enough that they still qualified for AFDC.[28]

than half agreed that recipients should do community service work in return for benefits.[29]

State legislatures have been a focal point of this pressure to transform welfare. Before the enactment of P.L. 104-193, 44 states had been granted waivers from federal law to test new approaches to transforming welfare into a work-based program. Lawmakers designed new approaches to eliminate work disincentives embedded in traditional welfare programs. Among the new approaches lawmakers pioneered were allowing recipients to keep more of their earnings, establishing responsibility contracts, and setting time limits and work requirements. By 1996, 28 states had already established immediate—or almost immediate—work participation requirements to transform welfare into a jobs program.[30]

In pursuing state-based welfare reforms, policymakers have focused on the critical role of child care. For example, before the 1996 congressional welfare debate, state legislatures had recognized the need for support services such as child care and health care for welfare recipients and those moving into the work force to become truly self-sufficient. Legislative welfare reform initiatives in **California**, **Massachusetts**, and **New Jersey** actually predated the Family Support Act of 1988 leading to that act's federal child care guarantee for AFDC recipients, as well as transitional child care (TCC) for up to one year for those leaving welfare for work. More recently, more than half the states expanded transitional child care services.

Today, states including **Minnesota**, **North Carolina**, and **Ohio** invest substantial state appropriations in a variety of child care or early childhood programs or for expansions of Head Start programs. In 1995, **Minnesota** increased funding by $16.2 million, or 86 percent.[31] To support its welfare program—the Family Investment Program—the **Iowa** legislature increased appropriations for child care by 62 percent from 1995 to 1996.[32] In 1996, 23 states increased appropriations for low-income child care or state preschool programs, or both.[33]

Between 1992 and 1996, 27 states requested waivers from federal welfare law to expand transitional child care services.[34] Most often this included allowing participants who leave welfare for work to receive child care help for longer periods than allowed under federal law. States also changed rules or procedures to make it easier for recipients to access services. In **Utah**, the state entirely eliminated time limits on child care assistance, instead linking coverage to income. **Connecticut** and **Montana** made similar changes in TCC policy.[35]

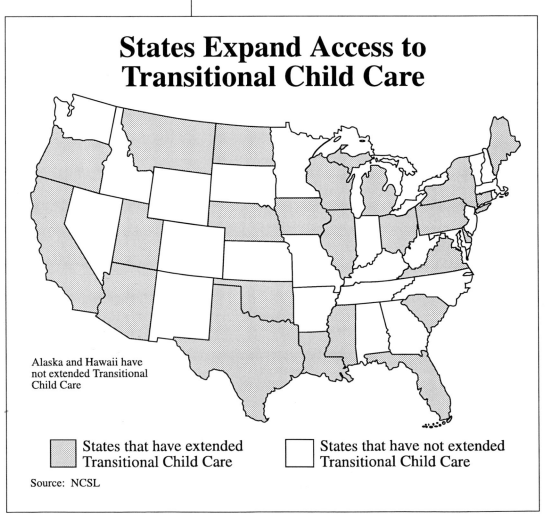

States Expand Access to Transitional Child Care

Alaska and Hawaii have not extended Transitional Child Care

☒ States that have extended Transitional Child Care

☐ States that have not extended Transitional Child Care

Source: NCSL

Many of these state welfare experiments have shown promising initial results in moving recipients into the work force, in expanding the number of welfare recipients who work, or increasing welfare families' incomes. In large part, such encouraging state experiences helped shape the federal welfare debate, culminating in the passage of P.L. 104-193. And under the new federal program, state policymakers assume an even greater leadership role.

Despite this remarkable legislative progress, experts suggest that there are significant problems with the nation's child care infrastructure. A growing body of research indicates that much of the nation's child care services are already of less-than-optimal quality. A recent multistate study found that the quality of child care is poor to mediocre in 86 percent of centers, with almost half the infants and toddlers in rooms of poor quality.[36] Another multistate study indicates that three out of every four low-income children have unsafe and unresponsive family and relative care.[37] Thirty-six states have waiting lists for subsidized care, some close to two years long and some containing 20,000 or 30,000 names.[38] The waiting lists indicate that affordable child care for the working poor—who are often one step away from welfare—is already scarce. And the increased child care demands under federal welfare reform may further stretch many states' capacities to serve both TANF recipients and the working poor.

TANF in Brief

The federal TANF legislation establishes a new structure for states' welfare programs. States now have considerable flexibility to change their welfare programs. In fact, the US Department of Health and Human Services directives on P.L. 104-193 are minimal in keeping with congressional intent to limit the federal agency's authority to direct state welfare activity. But the law is complex; it makes sweeping changes in more than 50 years of federal social welfare policy. Understanding its full implications for a state's work and training programs and related child care infrastructure demands in-depth knowledge of the law's provisions, the characteristics of the state's welfare population, existing state economic conditions and employment opportunities, and the scope, effectiveness, and availability of work programs and child care services.

A full discussion of the implications of P.L. 104-193 is beyond the scope of this book. Instead, this section offers a primer on TANF with an emphasis on the provisions most likely to affect the demand for child care.

TANF abolishes AFDC and essentially eliminates the cumbersome waiver process under which states previously had to pursue any major welfare reforms. The primary impact of the federal law on state child care services centers around two major areas. First, changes in the nature of the state-federal financing structure mean that states assume more fiscal responsibility for welfare programs. The new fiscal responsibility affects states' capacity to fund other state services, including child care programs. Second, work requirements, time limits, and other mandates of the federal law substantially affect child care demand in the states.

TANF Fiscal Structure

The federal legislation restructures federal financing so that states receive fixed amounts. Unlike AFDC, the federal block grants do not change as states' spending increases or decreases. Block grants shift the financial risk of welfare programs to the states. In effect, increases in welfare spending will be borne by state general fund revenues. On the other hand, any spending reductions achieved are completely savings for states, although the federal statute limits how much states can reduce their welfare spending.

The maintenance-of-effort provision requires states to maintain at least 80 percent of their 1994 spending on certain welfare expenditures. States that do not meet this requirement will lose a portion of their federal grant dollar for dollar during the subsequent year. The maintenance-of-effort requirement is reduced to 75 percent for states that meet work participation requirements. In addition, states that do not maintain 1994 spending 100 percent cannot access a contingency fund established to assist needy states with welfare funding during economic downturns.

The new financing structure increases the stakes for states as they plan TANF implementation. Policymakers must anticipate economic cycles that cause increases and decreases in public assistance caseloads and related spending. And they must pursue development of large-scale, effective work programs to enable recipients to support their families, reduce the effects of economic downturns, and maintain fiscal resources for other purposes in state budgets.

TANF Mandates

TANF imposes ambitious work-related mandates for the overhauled welfare system in an effort to transform welfare into a system providing transitional support that helps recipients find and keep jobs and become self-supporting. Three major mandates are to:

• Establish high targets for work and training program participation rates,

• Impose a two-year, work-related activity requirement, and

• Limit federally supported assistance to five years, with narrow exceptions.

The first mandate calls for immediate and progressive increases in available child care slots in the states to meet continuously rising work participation requirements. The work-related activity requirement means that states will face a big jump in child care demand when state or federal work requirements take effect. This will be two years hence for the federal provision and even earlier for states with more immediate requirements. The lifetime limit raises longer-term child care issues regarding potential support necessary to help families maintain self-sufficiency after five years. The following sections provide more details regarding these three TANF mandates.

Work Participation Requirements

Under the TANF program, states must place at least 25 percent of adult participants in work activities for a minimum of 20 hours during FY 1997. Work rates rise annually, peaking at 50 percent and 30 hours in FY 2002. Work requirements for two-parent families are considerably higher. Most states' work rates are reduced for declines in caseloads that have occurred since FY 1995. Compared with AFDC/JOBS, TANF limits the activities that count as work activity, particularly job search, job readi-

ness, and education. The statute specifies that providing child care to participants in community service programs can be considered a work activity.

WELFARE RECIPIENTS AS CHILD CARE WORKERS

Increasingly, state policymakers are exploring employment options for welfare recipients in the child care field to both employ recipients and increase child care supply. In addition, TANF specifies that providing child care is an allowable work activity. Professionals and advocates caution, however, that without supports and training, child care quality could be compromised. A recent study links better quality care with the desire to do the work and a professional interest in it.[39] This suggests that it is important to recruit recipients with a desire for careers in child care. In addition, the work is demanding, low paid, and often without benefits, all of which have implications if a major policy goal is to increase recipients' self-sufficiency.

Some states and communities have initiatives that recruit welfare recipients who want to provide care. These initiatives invest heavily in training and other supports to ensure quality care. Programs include recruitment and screening, training, career development, benefits, community supports, and activities that lead to professional licensure or other regulation.[40] **Colorado's** 1996 law establishes a pilot program of $25,000 grants to up to 10 agencies to recruit and train welfare recipients in child care careers. Under the legislation, grantees are required to help interested recipients in meeting applicable state licensing standards.[41]

States can exempt single parents with children under 1 from work requirements and exclude them from their rate calculations. The scarcity and high cost of infant and toddler day care should prompt most states to consider taking advantage of this one-time only option for mothers with very young children. In states such as **Colorado** and **Iowa**, monthly payments for certain infant and toddler care is larger than cash benefits.[42]

Unlike the AFDC/JOBS program, however, mothers with children over 1 cannot be excluded from the calculation of a states' work rate because of child care-related problems. But states can reduce required work hours for parents with children under 6; they have to work up to 20 hours per week, compared with up to 30 for parents with older children. States should consider taking advantage of this provision because of the increased flexibility to meet work requirements and the cost benefits. In states with relatively low cash assistance levels, such as **Mississippi** and **Texas**, average child care reimbursement rates are higher than monthly cash benefits.[43]

THE WORK MANDATE				
ALL FAMILIES (Single and Two-Parent Families)			TWO-PARENT FAMILIES	
FISCAL YEAR	PERCENT PARTICIPATION RATE	REQUIRED HOURS OF WORK PER WEEK	PERCENT PARTICIPATION RATE	REQUIRED HOURS OF WORK PER WEEK
1997	25	20	75	35
1998	30	20	75	35
1999	35	25	90	35
2000	40	30	90	35
2001	45	30	90	35
2002	50	30	90	35

Failure to meet work participation requirements results in a penalty of up to 5 percent of the state's block grant. The penalty increases by up to 2 percentage points each year the state fails to meet requirements, up to a maximum of 21 percent. In the initial program years, it will be easiest for states to fulfill work requirements. Credit for recent reductions in caseloads and the ability to count recipients' educational activities for a time make work rates more attainable early on. But the required rates increase progressively, and the time limits for counting recipients'educational activities expire. Especially if economic conditions worsen, it will be more difficult for states to meet the requirements in later years. States could incur financial penalties at a time when they are most in need of resources to pay benefits, create jobs, and provide child care.

Two-year Work Activity Requirement

Under the legislation, states must require adults receiving TANF assistance to engage in work after two years or earlier. States can exempt recipients from this requirement for good cause. States have substantial flexibility to define both "allowable work activities" and "good cause," but the federal law implicitly requires states to exempt parents of a child under 6 who cannot work because of certain child care-related problems. States must penalize individuals who fail to work as required, unless the

individual has a child under 6 and cannot work because of the lack of child care. The statute specifies distance, suitability and appropriateness, and affordability as factors to consider in determining whether child care is obtainable.

But most states will want to help parents quickly gain as much training and experience as possible to assist them in moving toward self-sufficiency within the new federal time limits. To help build recipients' experience while beefing up child care resources, for example, states could define a variety of child care-related experiences as allowable work activities. These include such activities as working in a Head Start program or helping out in an after school program.

Helping recipients gain experience quickly is also important because a number of states already impose more immediate work participation requirements than the new federal law. Most states had established their own time limits before the law was enacted. Twenty-eight states including **Florida**, **Oregon**, and **Wisconsin**, opted for short-term requirements (within six months) in their efforts to emphasize work. Other states have adopted time limits that require individuals to participate in work-related activities in exchange for benefits, most setting a 24-month limit like the federal law. As such requirements take effect, they substantially increase child care demand in the states. Consequently, many states' reforms include expansions in child care services to enable participants to enter and remain in the work force. A recent study of five state welfare demonstrations indicated that child care demand increased more rapidly than administrators had forecast.[44] Moreover, state welfare initiatives often allow broader exemptions than the federal law. Thus, most states have yet to face the full scope of increased demand likely to be generated by the federal requirements.

Wisconsin's recent experience is instructive here. Its new W-2 program includes work obligations for all adult recipients. Parents with children over 12 weeks must participate and even before the requirements have been fully implemented, the state has struggled with how to meet the increase in child care demand. By the time W-2 is fully operational in September, 1997, **Wisconsin** will more than triple to $185 million its investment in child care.[45] Among the major costs in the **Oregon** welfare program are those associated with child care and other support services. Today, the average cost for child care in

Oregon is $626 a month. Based on a sliding scale, a welfare recipient earning $5.50 per hour must contribute $71 and the state picks up $555. **Oregon** budgeted $10 million for child care in 1991, six years later the figure is estimated at ten times that amount.[46]

Five-year Time Limit on Cash Assistance

The federal legislation restricts states from using federal funds to pay cash assistance to families who have received TANF assistance for more than five years. This includes any child care paid for with TANF money. States can exempt up to 20 percent of the state's caseload from the five-year limit. States have the option to set even shorter lifetime limits. The limit is imposed regardless of whether a parent has a job or other income. To administer this and other time limits, many states will need to upgrade information systems and establish more sophisticated tracking procedures.

State-only funds can be used to provide benefits for families ineligible to receive federally supported aid because of the five-year limit. However, almost half of current recipients have received benefits for more than five years. The drain on state budgets to maintain families on state-only money will create considerable pressure for policymakers to move recipients into work activities that enable most families to be self-supporting before they reach their limits. Policymakers may also want to evaluate whether longer-term child care support will be

necessary for some families to maintain self-sufficiency beyond the five-year limits.

The federal law requires states to submit plans and transfer from AFDC to TANF by July 1, 1997. But post recession caseload and expenditure declines for AFDC in many states since 1995 created a financial incentive for immediate implementation. Because states receive TANF support based on their prior-year expenditures when caseloads were larger, almost all states receive more federal money initally under TANF. Consequently, most states submitted state plans within a month of the Oct. 1, 1996, starting date.

Generally, this initial executive-branch activity occurred without significant input from legislatures, most of which were not in session when the federal law was enacted. For the most part, governors' offices submitted plans to continue current programs or welfare waivers previously authorized by the legislatures. Generally, governors did not propose major changes in their welfare programs to comply with TANF. But most state welfare programs operate under statutes that can be changed only through the legislative process. Consequently, state legislatures will exert considerable influence over the implementation of TANF by virtue of their mandate to appropriate funds and make related policy decisions. State plans will require modification as policymakers begin to address more specific questions, including child care policies. It is important to note that approved state plans can be amended at any time, and it is likely that many will be with ongoing legislative input.

This rapid implementation resulted in increased federal money, but it also started the clock ticking on the work participation rate mandate, the two-year work activity requirement, and the five-year time limit. The new federal-state fiscal structure also creates considerable pressure for policymakers to move recipients into work activities that qualify for federal support after two years and into jobs so that families can be self-supporting before they reach their five-year limit. Recent state welfare initiatives give many jurisdictions a head start in restructuring their programs to comply

STATE WELFARE EXPENDITURES DECLINING

In recent years, AFDC caseloads have been declining substantially in most states. Nationwide the caseload dropped by 12 percent between July 1993 and July 1996. In 15 states, the reduction amounts to 20 percent or more. Correspondingly, overall state spending for welfare is also down. A recent NCSL fiscal survey found that states were spending $600 million, or 6.5 percent less on AFDC than they originally budgeted for FY 1996, even though the original FY 1996 appropriations were smaller than the previous year's expenditures. AFDC allocations are estimated to account for 2.2 percent of state general fund budgets in FY 97, down from 2.6 percent the previous year. Nationwide, AFDC spending has dropped by more than 10 percent in the past two years. In four states, however, AFDC caseloads have actually increased, led by a 14 percent rise in **Hawaii**. States with increasing caseloads are in the toughest position for implementing new federal welfare block grants.[47]

with the federal law, but all will need to move quickly through the legislative process to establish large-scale employment programs in order to meet the TANF work mandates.

These new work programs require additional spending, but the TANF block grants do not include supplementary funds for them. The Congressional Budget Office (CBO) projects that the additional costs for states to meet work requirements will rise from $370 million in 1997 to $4 billion six years later. CBO predicts that if states maintain historical spending patterns, the work programs will be underfunded by $13 billion over the six-year program. For many states, the actual cost of new work programs exceeds the federal penalty for failing to meet work requirements, leading the CBO to predict that most states will opt to absorb the federal penalties.[48]

Many welfare experts concur that states will struggle to develop new programs and find the financing needed to meet the TANF requirements, particularly in economic downturns. Some argue that states will be forced to transfer funds from other block grant services—particularly cash assistance—to meet the work requirements. Others believe that the reforms provide the vehicle for successful implementation. States will benefit from reduced federal paperwork and administration and new flexibility to fashion state-specific programs and to set most eligibility rules and benefit levels.

Substantial increases in the programs to provide child care to enable recipients to work are critical for successful implementation of TANF. The federal legislation provided increased funding for the child care block grant. This interaction between the TANF block grant and the Child Care and Development Block Grant is discussed in more detail in the next section.

The Child Care and Development Block Grant

Beginning in October 1996, Title VI of P.L. 104-193 consolidated three welfare-related federal funding streams into a single child care program as a block grant to the states. The law abolished child care programs formerly known as Title IV-A AFDC, Transitional Child Care, and At-Risk Child Care. The law combines them with the existing Child Care and Development Block Grant (CCDBG) for administration by the lead state agency under the CCDBG. In general, the provisions of current CCDBG law, including health and safety protections, apply to the new combined fund, referred to by HHS as the Child Care and Development Fund.

Total funding for the new consolidated program is $19.85 billion over six years, or approximately $3.5 billion more in "capped entitlement" funding than the states spent in 1995. The new child care block grant includes three types of funding: mandatory, matching, and discretionary.

Under the new funding scheme, states get a mandatory base amount of federal funds that approximates the total amount each state received previously under the three Title IV-A funding streams. Allocation of the mandatory base portion is set at the higher of 1992-94 average, 1994 spending, or 1995 spending. No match is required to access these federal funds, which total $7.2 billion for the six-year program.

Additional funds above the mandatory base amount are available on a matching basis for states that meet two requirements. First, a state must obligate all mandatory funds allocated to it during that fiscal year. Second, states must maintain 100 percent maintenance-of-effort for recent nonfederal child care expenditures. In short, to access the "new" federal matching funds, most states must not just continue to invest in child care at their historic spending levels but also provide additional matching funds. States that meet these two requirements are eligible to receive their share of $3.5 billion in additional federal capped entitlement funds for child care at FY 1995 Medicaid matching rates. State allocations for the these funds are based on the same formula as under the previous At-Risk Child Care program. Funds are distributed according to the state's percentage of the nation's population of children under 13.

Both the mandatory and matching child care funds described above are provided as a capped entitlement to the states; amounts are automatically appropriated and are guaranteed to eligible states but not to individuals within them. States, however, are required to spend 70 percent of these child care allocations on families receiving TANF, or for those who are leaving or are at risk of going on the program.

In building their child care infrastructure, states also continue to get a portion of the $6 billion authorized for the next six years under the Child Care and Development Block Grant. This is slightly more than previously provided under the CCDBG, but it is subject to annual appropriations and, as such, is not guaranteed in the same sense as "capped entitlement" funding. No match is required to access the discretionary funds that are allocated according to the existing CCDBG formula. Taken together, the entitlement and discretionary child care dollars are estimated to increase the federal child care funding available to states particularly in the first years of the program. All states that take full advantage of the program receive increases in federal child care funds from their 1996 allocations. Increases range from $107.5 million, or up 131 percent, for **California** to $585,000, or less than a 1 percent increase, for **New Jersey**. States must obligate their child care money by the end of the fiscal year, and unobligated funds will be redistributed to other states based on their proportion of children under age 13. Although states cannot transfer CCDBG funds to any other block grant, they can transfer up to 30 percent of their TANF funds to the child care block grant.[49]

Athough states will receive more federal child care funding in the first years of the new block grant than they were expected to get under the previous system, questions remain about the adequacy of federal funding over the long term for all priority populations. CBO projects that the costs of providing child care to participants in work programs under P.L. 104-193 will be $1.5 billion in 1997, rising to almost $5 billion by the sixth year of the program. According to CBO estimates, the additional federal child care allocations are adequate for states to provide child care for work program participants. But resources are insufficient if states want to meet both work requirements and maintain current spending for the working poor and those making the transition off welfare. In fact, states wishing to adequately serve all three populations face a $1.4 billion shortfall during the six-year period.[50] Additionally,

since many states use the Social Services Block Grant to fund child care services, recent reductions in that appropriation of 11 percent may further squeeze states' child care budgets.

Some child care experts worry that states will be forced to limit child care resources to assist working poor families in maintaining financial independence and staying off the rolls. In addition, transitional child care support to assist parents in leaving—and staying off—welfare may be compromised to meet the demand for work-related child care. Thus, increased demand for child care could create significant pressure to spread existing resources even thinner, potentially risking the quality of publicly provided child care services even further.

THE CHILD AND ADULT CARE FOOD PROGRAM

The new federal welfare law included cuts and other revisions in the Child and Adult Care Food Program (CACFP). Funding was cut by $2.3 billion over six years in CACFP, an entitlement program providing nutrition-related reimbursement to certain care providers, including child care providers serving low-income populations. Chief among these changes is the establishment of a means test for some family homes. Tier I providers continue to receive current reimbursement levels for meals served. These providers include those located within neighborhoods where at least 50 percent of families have incomes under 185 percent of the poverty level. Homes operated by a provider whose family income is below that level are also reimbursed at current rates. Tier II providers can opt to implement a means test for receipt of full reimbursement for children with low incomes and reduced rates for children from higher income families. They can choose not to establish a means test and receive significantly reduced rates for all meals served. The Tier II rates are reduced from 86 cents, $1.75, and 47 cents to 27 cents, 95 cents, and 13 cents for breakfast, lunch, and snack, respectively. The legislation appropriates $5 million for one-time grants to states to help implement the means test. Other provisions include a reduction in the inflation adjustment for all family child care homes and elimination of reimbursement for an additional snack or meal served to children in centers for more than eight hours. States are no longer required to conduct outreach for the program. Child care experts caution that these changes may affect not only the supply of child care for low-income children, but also the quality of care. Participation in the program provided additional incentives for providers to obtain licensure, and CACFP personnel offered supplemental support and oversight of participating providers, many of whom may now simply find it easier to drop out of the program.[51]

STATE CHILD CARE ALLOCATIONS

	FY1996	FY1997	Increase
Alabama	$16,340,975	$27,538,930	$11,197,955
Alaska	4,628,222	5,573,564	945,342
Arizona	24,802,279	32,654,444	7,852,165
Arkansas	5,216,653	11,928,191	6,711,538
California	81,595,011	189,109,830	107,514,819
Colorado	11,935,519	20,458,829	8,523,310
Connecticut	25,860,821	27,297,695	1,436,874
Delaware	5,544,948	7,097,533	1,534,585
D.C.	3,984,787	6,007,129	2,022,342
Florida	48,138,526	78,991,515	30,852,989
Georgia	48,944,950	56,725,095	7,780,145
Hawaii	6,246,320	8,544,528	2,298,208
Idaho	2,836,570	6,360,048	3,523,478
Illinois	83,741,735	92,635,041	8,893,306
Indiana	37,685,927	41,476,175	3,790,248
Iowa	6,476,450	16,176,667	9,700,217
Kansas	10,166,728	16,962,947	6,796,219
Kentucky	17,289,150	26,565,371	9,276,221
Louisiana	12,716,209	26,579,410	13,863,201
Maine	3,026,858	6,253,341	3,226,483
Maryland	23,045,304	36,968,426	13,923,122
Massachusetts	55,880,580	60,349,955	4,469,375
Michigan	41,192,696	58,298,700	17,106,005
Minnesota	26,728,107	36,230,664	9,502,557
Mississippi	9,599,538	14,049,912	4,450,374
Missouri	27,599,568	38,926,173	11,326,605
Montana	3,626,693	5,561,904	1,935,211
Nebraska	7,786,148	15,877,705	8,091,557
Nevada	3,499,702	6,878,492	3,378,790
New Hampshire	4,362,499	8,153,892	3,791,393
New Jersey	52,052,690	52,638,058	585,368
New Mexico	8,707,301	13,916,036	5,208,735
New York	117,110,636	153,480,403	36,369,767
N. Carolina	66,882,817	88,590,381	21,707,564
N. Dakota	1,708,379	4,226,635	2,528,256
Ohio	68,441,868	100,003,527	31,561,659
Oklahoma	30,998,199	33,904,916	2,906,717
Oregon	23,335,244	27,598,040	4,262,796
Pennsylvania	59,244,874	85,648,280	26,403,406
Rhode Island	7,119,676	9,159,194	2,039,518
S. Carolina	13,300,903	19,673,401	6,372,498
S. Dakota	1,932,447	3,805,883	1,873,436
Tennessee	47,643,844	51,258,743	3,614,899
Texas	73,324,512	116,877,750	43,553,238
Utah	12,181,102	19,428,168	7,247,066
Vermont	3,208,151	5,666,584	2,458,433
Virginia	21,880,669	38,380,459	16,499,790
Washington	38,002,711	56,766,466	18,763,755
West Virginia	9,726,862	12,973,006	3,246,144
Wisconsin	35,205,439	38,370,188	3,164,749
Wyoming	2,347,399	4,162,277	1,814,878
Total	**$1,354,855,195**	**$1,922,742,500**	**$567,887,305**

Source: U.S. Department of Health and Human Services. Includes welfare related child care, not discretionary.

Under the new federal law, states must allocate at least 4 percent of their child care funds for improving quality, expanding the supply, and providing consumer education. States should carefully consider whether to maintain or increase spending on quality enhancements and supply building, especially in the initial program years. An early investment allows states to upgrade the quality of their child care infrastructures before the TANF work requirements rise to peak levels demanding proportionally greater spending on services. One-time investments in quality, can reap long-term benefits. These investments might include developing training materials, building provider support networks, preparing peer trainers, expanding resource and referral, leveraging private sector support, and establishing recruitment initiatives especially for scarce types of care like care for school-age or sick children, or for parents who work off-hour shifts. This strategy has the added advantage of helping states achieve the spending levels required to qualify for all new federal child care funding.

Under the new child care block grant, administrative costs are limited to 5 percent of a state's child care fund, but several activities are specifically defined as nonadministrative and are therefore not included within the administrative limit. These activities include eligibility determination, preparation for and participation in judicial hearings, child care placement, recruitment, licensing, inspection, placement supervision, rate-setting, resource and referral services, training, and development and maintenance of computer information systems.

Under P.L. 104-193, states are prohibited from using federal funds to provide services for new legal immigrants for the first five years after their arrival in the country. It is unclear at this writing, however, whether and how this provision applies to the provision of child care services. Child nutrition programs—including the Child and Adult Care Food Program—and Head Start are exempt from immigrant restrictions. These restrictions do not apply to certain "refugees" including Cuban and Haitian entrants.

Clearly, policymakers are faced with critical choices in implementing the Child Care Block Grant. These policy and fiscal decisions that will determine resource allocation and programming are critical to the success of state welfare reform efforts and will affect service delivery systems for years to come. Legislators must take a thoughtful planning approach to their child care and welfare strategies at the state level, acknowledging the interrelationships between the policy goals of family self-sufficiency, access to affordable quality care, and outcomes for children. Some of the decisions legislators may be faced with are discussed in the next section.

Critical Child Care and Welfare Policy Choices

Overview

The additional work obligations for welfare clients mandated under the federal law create significant new pressures to increase supply and to do so quickly. But a two-generation strategy demands that policymakers increase child care slots thoughtfully, with an eye toward the children who will be spending considerable amounts of time in them. To be sure, welfare reforms that increase family self-sufficiency and income, reduce the number of children raised in welfare poverty, and augment parents' self-esteem through work will reap significant benefits for children in welfare families. Policymakers will want to assure that these benefits are not offset by placing large numbers of welfare children in unsafe or unresponsive care arrangements that compromise their development.

Yet the decisions lawmakers face in addressing quality are not new. Lawmakers, in fact, have been deliberating and establishing policies to assure quality services for years. The major change in the current environment is integrating these policies in an era of significantly increased child care demand and rising state fiscal responsibility for welfare programs.

Among the important decisions over which state legislators exert considerable influence are those related to strategic planning, the appropriation of state funds to maximize federal support, funding mechanisms and reimbursement policies, targeting populations for services, and regulation. Taken together, these imminent decisions will determine the future course of state child care systems and ultimately whether state policy supports work force development and child development as complementary—not competing—goals.

Planning

Effective Oct. 1, 1996, states began receiving their child care funding allotments after their CCDBG lead agency completed an interim application. Lead agencies also must conduct a thorough and inclusive planning process—including a public hearing—to develop a comprehensive two-year state child care plan and final application for submission to HHS by July 1, 1997. State child care plans are required every two years.

This plan is separate from that required for states to implement TANF as discussed in previous sections. But, because of the obvious interrelationships between TANF and the Child Care and Development Block Grant, these plans should be considered in tandem. State lawmakers can help assure that these two planning efforts are coordinated. Too often in the past, state child care administrators, private service providers, and other child care stakeholders have not been integrally involved in overall state welfare planning efforts despite the role of child care in ensuring the success of welfare efforts. Legislators themselves may also want to participate in the planning process and monitor it to ensure statewide input and citizen and stakeholder participation and to coordinate planning and funding efforts for child care and TANF.

Maximizing Funds

Almost immediately lawmakers must make a very basic decision about the state child care budget: whether to maximize federal funding available to the state. To do so may require the expenditure of state funds beyond historical spending patterns.

As discussed in the previous section, all states are eligible to receive more federal money than they received in 1996. However, to access all additional federal dollars, states must meet three requirements. First, they must obligate all the federal funds provided through their basic mandatory allot-

ments. Generally, this is an amount equal to their historical federal support for Title IV-A child care. Second, states must maintain a 100 percent maintenance-of-effort for certain welfare-related child care expenditures, that is, they must invest in welfare-related child care at the same level as they have in the past.

According to HHS, what counts as state match includes only the types of services that were previously allowed under the Title IV-A child care programs. These services were limited in scope and did not include expenditures for licensing, training, and quality-enhancing activities. But these expenditures and others such as appropriations for prekindergarten programs may—pending federal regulations—be used as match to draw down additional federal support. Once a 100 percent maintenance-of-effort is achieved, states must provide a

BUILD CHILD CARE BY LEVERAGING PRIVATE SECTOR SUPPORT

In its guidelines for state planning, HHS recommends soliciting the help of the business community. States and communities should consider using some of their new child care funds to engage the business community in helping to build child care funds that will grow over time. Public dollars can be used to establish a "Working Parent Assistance Trust Fund" in a community or state. Corporations could be challenged to donate resources to this fund which in turn would help improve the supply of quality services for the total community or provide targeted scholarships to help families pay for care.[52]

State legislatures have already begun this effort. **Florida's** 1996 omnibus welfare law established a state child care executive partnership to encourage employer and foundation support for child care for working families. The law establishes a $2 million state pool to match dollar for dollar funding from the private sector. The fund will provide subsidies for low-income working parents.[53]

In **Colorado**, a 1995 business commission on child care recommended a number of ways to involve corporations in ensuring that all families have access to quality and affordable child care.[54] These included establishing a multi-bank community development corporation to provide loans and other financial assistance to child care providers, developing and distributing a business resource guide on child care employee options, distributing information on model child care programs that employers can adapt, and creating a permanent business and child care commission. A year later, a public/private partnership was formed to guide the community development corporation. Funding is being sought from financial institutions throughout the state.[55]

match at the Medicaid matching rates for fiscal year 1995 to receive all the federal capped entitlement funding for which they are eligible.

States may choose to invest less in child care, but in doing so may receive less federal money to build their child care infrastructure as welfare-related child care demand rises. Unused funds will be redistributed to other states. States who chose not to access matching federal funds one year may become eligible again by subsequently meeting the basic requirements.

Who to Serve

Decisions about who to serve in state child care programs will affect the short- and long-term demand. Federal welfare-related money must be used primarily for parents involved with the state TANF program. At least 70 percent of the funds must be used to support TANF participants and those leaving the program, or at risk of going on the program.

States can choose to exempt single adult parents with children under age 1 from the work requirements, thus reducing the need for expensive publicly subsidized infant and toddler care. States that impose immediate work requirements for participants with very young children—such as **Florida**, **Nebraska**, **Michigan**, **Oregon**, and **Wisconsin**—will need to plan child care expenditures accordingly. Mothers with children under age six cannot be sanctioned if they cannot work due to child care problems. But these mothers must be counted in state work rate calculations with the exception of those with very young children. This creates an incentive to employ them, rather than exempt them. In addition, states will want to help parents get the experience necessary to advance toward self-sufficiency before they reach their lifetime limits on assistance. Clearly, policy decisions regarding who to exempt and when to impose work requirements affect both the timing and scope of additional child care demand in the state.

Decisions about whether to continue a state's investment in transitional care and services for the working poor may have longer-term but important consequences. As outlined in previous sections, state welfare reform experiences now suggest that transitional child care is critical to helping welfare mothers get and keep jobs. This experience prompted more than half the states to expand the availability of transitional care

beyond federal limits in recent years. Budget planning will be necessary to continue transitional services for families currently leaving welfare and to expand long-term support for parents who reach their federal or earlier state-imposed lifetime limits on assistance.

In addition, lawmakers will want to deliberate policies regarding ongoing child care support for the working poor, who are often one step away from welfare. Large waiting lists in 36 states suggest that such care is already in short supply.[56] This type of support, however, may be necessary to ensure that these families remain self-sufficient and are not forced on to the welfare rolls. And if state welfare programs move more families into primarily entry-level jobs without benefits, the demand for child care support is likely to increase.

CBO estimates indicate that federal child care support over the long haul is insufficient to meet both the work requirements for TANF participants *and* to maintain current state investments for child care for those in transition and the working poor. But the CBO predicts that the child care funds are adequate for states to meet work-related child care requirements.[57] State policymakers may want to consider targeting any expansions in state child care funding to maintain and augment services for the working poor. In addition, policymakers may want to examine how other state programs, such as preschool or Head Start, can be better utilized to fill some of the needs of poor working parents and those leaving welfare. For example, states can provide incentives for Head Start programs to expand their hours to meet the needs of working parents.

How to Reimburse

Decisions about reimbursement affect both the supply and quality of child care service. States now have more flexibility to determine reimbursement levels and make related decisions. The new federal law requires states to outline the mechanism used to determine provider payment levels and to ensure equal access to services, but it no longer requires the use of a market survey or payment at certain levels. Nonetheless, supply may dwindle in states that reduce their rates far below what the market will bear. More important, adequate reimbursement is critical in the effort to maintain a two-generation child care strategy that achieves both work force and child development goals. Research indicates that quality costs in the short term, but it pays off big in the long term. A recent study of child care cost, quality, and child outcomes, however, found that the cost of providing care at higher quality centers was only about 10 percent higher compared with those of average quality.[58] Policymakers will need to give considerable thought to the consequences of reducing payment levels markedly in an effort to spread resources further. At the least, providers and other stakeholders should be included in the decision making process.

Under the previous system, the Child Care and Development Block Grant (CCDBG) was targeted to families earning less than 75 percent of the state median income (SMI). The new law raises the maximum eligibility level to 85 percent of SMI, and states have an opportunity to structure their child care programs in ways that best fit their needs. Federal officials suggest using one income level as the eligibility standard for all child care assistance in order to streamline administration of funds. Under **Wisconsin**'s new welfare program, any family earning less than 165 percent of the federal poverty level (FPL) is eligible for child care.

The federal law allows states to continue to use the "income disregard" as a payment mechanism under the TANF program. Under AFDC states could reimburse parents indirectly for child care expenses by not counting up to $200 in monthly income when calculating cash benefit levels. Many states used this option to reimburse welfare recipients in work and training programs. States are free to use the child care disregard under the TANF program and to set the disregard amounts. Child care stakeholders complain that the disregard amounts set in the past are problematic because they fail to cover the actual cost of care. In addition, use of the income disregard means that states will need to operate two separate child care programs—one under TANF and the other through the child care block grant.

An additional consideration in using the income disregard under TANF is that all services provided to individuals are subject to the other TANF requirements, including work-related and lifetime limits and work requirements. Child care provided through the block grant mechanism is not subject to these requirements and is considerably more flexible. For example, individuals could receive child care support beyond the limits under the Child Care Block Grant and states do not need to track

individuals for purposes of imposing those limits. This is one of reasons for states to consider transferring funds from TANF to other block grants as allowed under the federal law. Up to 30 percent of the TANF block grant can be transferred to the CCDBG.

To promote quality, several states have chosen to pay a higher rate to providers who meet certain regulatory standards. Under its new law, **Florida** pays regulated providers at the prevailing market rate and unregulated providers at 50 percent of the market rate. **Wisconsin** now pays untrained family child care providers at 50 percent of the market rate compared to 75 percent of the rate for family child care providers who get training. Similarly, states such as **Ohio** and **Maine** have authorized higher reimbursement rates for providers who meet national child care standards.

The federal law encourages states to facilitate parental choice; it requires the use of sliding fee scales for parents; but related decisions also affect parental choices. To date, most states base their sliding fee scales on parents' income. Experts suggest that poor mothers should have to devote no more than 10 percent of family income for child care.[59] Policies requiring poor parents to pay based on the type of care, rather than income, may preclude their ability to choose certain types, such as center-based care. States will also want to consider how fast the fee scale rises with income. Rapidly rising parental liabilities with small increases in income can push a mother off the "cliff" and back on welfare.

State Examples

Illinois

To create incentives to "make work pay," the **Illinois** General Assembly in 1993 approved significant changes related to child care as part of a larger welfare reform package. One change was in response to a study of 7,000 AFDC recipients, conducted by the Department of Public Aid, which identified the child care disregard as a major barrier to employment because it failed to adequately cover the real market costs of child care for working families. According to the report, "the disregard penalizes families' first steps towards real financial independence by requiring them to incur hundreds of dollars in child care costs the moment they begin working."[60] In the program's first month, the number of AFDC families with earned income rose 20 percent, compared with the usual 6 percent increase for that month. Eight months after these changes were enacted, the number of working AFDC families in the state had risen 58 percent to 22,469.[61]

The initiative replaces the income disregard with direct payments to providers for child care and allows parents to keep $2 out of every $3 earned until their earned income reaches approximately three times their cash grant level. At that point, the person is no longer eligible for welfare but can automatically receive transitional child care (TCC) benefits.[62] Moreover, the legislature appropriated $18 million to implement the change, which contributed to a 50 percent increase in the number of working AFDC families.[63]

Two years later in December 1995, the percentage of working welfare families had more than doubled, to nearly 17 percent. By this time 97 of **Illinois'** 102 counties had at least 20 percent of their welfare caseload working, compared with only eight counties before the program. Chicago's Cook County was one of the five counties below the 20 percent mark. The state's overall caseload has dropped by one-third since the program began.[64]

Illinois' most recent study of welfare families revealed that many families leave welfare for jobs with irregular hours. Nearly three-quarters of the 207 TCC recipients studied worked shifts outside of regular daytime hours. Of these nearly one-third worked weekends, one-quarter worked weekends and nights, and others had a variety of schedules, including nights only. Consequently, the state is working to expand child care options for parents with irregular work schedules.[65]

Now **Illinois** is examining its entire child care system. State officials are considering expanding child care coverage to all families under a certain income level, such as between 40 percent and 60 percent of the state median income. Another option being considered is to require all parents to pay a fee according to their income. In addition, state officials are examining how to distribute quality enhancement grants, especially to facilitate higher provider salaries.[66]

These **Illinois** child care changes will be given greater focus within the context of the state's current administrative reorganization. Child care issues will be removed from the state Departments of Children and Family Services (DCFS) and Public Aid (DPA) and placed in a new Department of Human Services, where welfare reform and child care issues will be more prominent. The DCFS will become mainly a child welfare agency, and the DPA will handle only Medicaid and child support issues.[67]

Iowa

In 1993 the **Iowa** General Assembly passed a welfare reform package called the Family Investment Plan (FIP). The program is unique because it is crafted to each family. Clients sign a family investment agreement, participate in work training, and leave AFDC by a mutually agreed-upon date. There is some flexibility to adjust the plan in special circumstances.[68]

As part of this strategy, the legislature took a significant step toward advancing self-sufficiency by expanding transitional child care (TCC) coverage from 12 to 24 months.[69] The state was one of the first to enact this extension; recently 26 other states have also extended TCC coverage. Later, the state also expanded TCC in other ways, such as allowing those who get child support and those who leave welfare voluntarily to gain eligibility. A study of FIP by Mathematica Policy Research Inc. found that the number of participants with earnings increased from 18 percent in September 1993 to 33 percent in September 1995.[70] **Iowa** has submitted a state plan to continue the FIP program—including its child care provisions—under the new TANF program.

In addition to taking the lead on issues such as work requirements and TCC expansions, **Iowa** policymakers have also addressed the child care demand issue. Beginning in 1995, **Iowa's** legislators required the state to prioritize child care services for the neediest populations. The first group targeted for child care assistance are the poorest families on cash assistance who work at least 30 hours per week. Other priority populations include young parents in employment, education, or training; low-income families with a child with special needs; and low-income families working parttime. The state also raised income eligibility from 100 percent to 110 percent of the federal poverty level for families working at least 30 hours per week.[71]

In 1996 legislators backed up their welfare policy with a 62 percent increase in subsidized child care funds, an additional $4.8 million. Because of the impact of the state's welfare initiatives on child care services, the legislature required the state to explore changes in specific child care financing policies. These policies are those many states will be addressing under TANF: payment rates and mechanisms, quality enhancements, copayment systems, and child care during nonstandard hours. The law requires the state to look into higher reimbursement rates for providers caring for at least 75 percent publicly funded children and the policy implications for enhanced reimbursement for registered family child care homes.[72] The state has established a task force to consider these and other policy changes, such as elimination of the FIP child care disregard, increasing the number of providers for families working weekends and second shifts, better coordination of funds, and sliding fee scale adjustments. By addressing these key issues, Iowa officials expect to develop a comprehensive child care plan, with broad input, to submit to the federal government.[73]

IOWA'S FAMILY DEVELOPMENT AND SELF-SUFFICIENCY GRANT PROGRAM

In addition to FIP, **Iowa** also operates a program for welfare recipients at risk of long-term welfare dependency through its family development and self-sufficiency grant program, FaDSS. The program addresses the child development needs of children of long-term welfare recipients, as well as other issues relating to moving toward self-sufficiency. FaDSS grant programs provide family development and advocacy for participant families and may include: parent-child relationships, parent education and support with child care assistance, and budget, education, and other family needs. A 1995 evaluation of FaDSS found that participants increased their knowledge and skills, helping them reach self-sufficiency. Compared to a control group, FaDSS participants made specific improvements in education and training, finding employment, job satisfaction, wages, benefits, housing and family needs, self-confidence and overall competency. The report notes that, despite the achievements, participants moved slower off welfare than policymakers would like to see. After two years, only 30 percent were economically independent. It took 3 and a half years for half to permanently leave AFDC. The study's results, however, indicate that FaDSS is succeeding at its goal of long-term self-sufficiency, as more participants than non-participants left welfare after five years.[74]

Utah

In the early 1990s, the **Utah** Legislature, in cooperation with the state Department of Human Services, made substantial changes in the welfare system. The agency initiated a new demonstration project, the Single Parent Employment Program (SPED), in three jurisdictions to begin changing AFDC/JOBS to an employment-focused program. To support welfare parents in making the transition to work, the plan includes a significant child care component. The state has been expanding the program, previously approved through federal waivers. Under TANF, the program will go statewide by adding two local jurisdictions.

Since the program's implementation in 1993, legislators have recognized the importance of child care to the welfare reform program and have acted to improve quality and expand child care services for participants. Utah policymakers have addressed one of the key issues in implementing the new federal welfare law: provider payment rates. Because child care reimbursement rates were relatively low, the Legislature required the state to create a different payment method. The result was a system that pays parents upfront instead of reimbursing parents after child care is provided (and that allows higher payments). Under TANF, **Utah** plans to continue using the market-rate survey system to ensure that welfare families have access to a wide range of child care services. State officials also report that parents have more choice under the new system.[75]

Last year, legislators required that SPED be expanded statewide by June 1997.[76] Evaluation results of the program, now called the Family Employment Program, are impressive. The 1996 Kearns site evaluation revealed that of the 481 families in the program, only 14 percent were still receiving cash assistance and not working two years later. Over half received no public assistance, a quarter were receiving only Medicaid and food stamps, and another 10 percent were working while on cash assistance. Other program sites have experienced similar successes. In addition, since 1993 the state's caseload has declined by 44 percent and grant expenditures are also down 46 percent.[77]

The project has saved money in cash assistance and food stamp benefits; however, expenses in other areas have increased. Because program resources are dedicated to self-sufficiency, costs for case management, employment, and education are twice as expensive as similar costs under the old welfare program. In addition, child care costs at the demonstration sites were 50 percent higher largely because more clients are employed or participating in training and education activities. State administrators are finding that child care costs are rising by approximately 30 percent as the program nears statewide expansion. With statewide implementation expected this year, **Utah** officials expect child care demand to continue to rise under TANF.[78]

POVERTY IN THE UNITED STATES

The number of families living in poverty in the United States was increasing in the 1980s, but has began to show a slight decrease. The proportion of poor children rose from 14 percent in 1969 to nearly 22 percent in 1991, dropping to 20 percent in 1995. But poverty rates for young children (under 6) are higher than for all children: one-quarter live in poverty. Overall, young children are the nation's poorest age group. For African American children and children of Hispanic origin, the figures are still worse: 49 percent of African American children and 42 percent of children of Hispanic origin live in poverty. The poverty rate for families with children is 16 percent. Poverty rates are over twice as high for African American and Hispanic American families, at 34 percent and 33 percent respectively.

Many people who work are still poor. In 1995, 67 percent of families headed by a female had wage income, but 28 percent of those families still remained in poverty. Forty percent of African American families and families of Hispanic origin remained in poverty even with a wage earner in the family.[79] For low-wage, unskilled workers, the challenge of earning more than the poverty level may be unrealistic. Working full time at the minimum wage of $4.75 per hour amounts to an annual income of $9,120, or approximately $6,480 less than the 1996 federal poverty of level for a family of four.[80] It is this population of U.S. citizens who are referred to as the "working poor."

State Actions to Coordinate Child Care Programs and Funding

A benefit of the new federal approach to child care and welfare reform is the elimination of separate categorical federal child care programs, each with a different objective. Too often, categorical funding streams "unintentionally segment the low-income population into categories that fail to recognize the similarity of their economic circumstances and child care needs," according to a GAO report.[81] States now have the opportunity to streamline the multiple programs and funding streams for child care, which has fiscal and program implications for both states and families.

Several states began coordination efforts even before passage of the federal law. **New Jersey**'s law authorizes a single sliding fee scale and eligibility requirements for all state programs.[82]

Kentucky passed a law that required all child care programs administered by the state to use the same eligibility application, provider agreements, and payment levels and methods for similar services regardless of the public funding source.[83] The **California** Legislature allowed families who lose eligibility for one subsidized child care program to continue to receive services from the same provider if they are enrolled in another program, promoting continuity of services.[84] **Maine** legislators required a single application form for most child care programs,[85] and a 1991 **Ohio** law simplifies application procedures.[86]

Florida

Florida's lawmakers made major strides in 1996 in coordinating state welfare goals with the broader early childhood education system. In the state's omnibus welfare law, legislators required that 75 percent of prekindergarten program enrollees be economically disadvantaged 4-year-old children of working parents or parents in the welfare reform program. The law requires the state to consider local child care waiting lists in the calculation of allocations of prekindergarten funds to school districts. Recognizing the full-day needs of working parents, the law also requires local school districts, child care agencies, Head Start programs, and private preschool providers to assess preschool children who are eligible for subsidized child care to identify those needing an extended day and year program. The law further requires school districts to enter into collaborative agreements with publicly funded early childhood programs to ensure compliance with standards and to maximize resources. The coordination efforts are strengthened by a mandated single point of entry for all publicly supported early childhood programs.[87]

Conclusion

With the advent of federal welfare reform, state lawmakers face formidable challenges in implementing a two-generational child care strategy—one that meets the needs of children for quality programming to improve their long-term outcomes, while also meeting parents immediate needs for care to enable them to work.

The new child care block grant and related welfare legislation ends the federal entitlement to child care established under the 1988 Family Support Act for working welfare recipients, those in work and training programs, and those who leave welfare for work. Instead, P.L. 104-193 consolidates four federal child care funding streams, increases initial allocations above expected funding levels under the previous system, and leaves more discretion to the states to fashion child care programs that support successful welfare reform.

States have considerable flexibility in fashioning child care programs to meet new demands created by the work requirements of the law, but in the long term they will be doing so with federal resources that may not address new demands for all priority populations. Yet Congress did recognize the importance of child care funding to the success of welfare reform and provided supplementary resources for child care, especially compared with work program mandates that were not given additional funding. And the integration of federal funding streams offers a significant opportunity for states to streamline and consolidate child care services to

achieve administrative efficiency. It removes a number of federal rules and regulations, such as the time limits on transitional child care, that have sometimes hindered state efforts to move recipients into jobs. Indeed, increased demand for child care resulting from the law could serve as an impetus for states to better coordinate welfare-related child care programs with state preschool and Head Start services to maximize resources for the influx of welfare recipients with new work obligations. As states consider how to implement both TANF and the child care block grant, a number of pioneering state initiatives can help them to consider both work force and child development policy goals.

CHAPTER 8

EARLY CARE AND FAMILY SUPPORT

Introduction

Policymakers across the nation—whether male or female, conservative or liberal, leadership or rank and file—are concerned about families. Family advocates in state legislatures recognize that past policy approaches, often based on categorical legislative structures, are inadequate to meet the broad-based needs of families today. Rather than creating yet another categorical program in response to yet another symptom of family dysfunction, pioneering legislators are experimenting with family support policy approaches. These are strategies that cut across narrow committee jurisdictions to offer families comprehensive, flexible and concrete help designed to support parents, alleviate social isolation and improve overall family functioning.

Previous chapters in this book have focused on early care and education in a variety of specific legislative jurisdictions. This one will focus on how early care and education cut across jurisdictions and will highlight their role in the larger family support movement. Early care and education are, in fact, critical components in promising cross-jurisdictional initiatives to address the needs of today's families more effectively.

The chapter describes both the multifaceted, interrelated problems facing all families today and those facing especially vulnerable families, with particular emphasis on their child care concerns. It analyzes existing systems of family service delivery as a foundation for new approaches. In addition, the chapter discusses the nature of the family support movement, the research base for it and institutional barriers—including those in the legislative process itself—to implementing family support reforms. It provides examples of family support initiatives in several state legislatures and case

studies of comprehensive initiatives in **North Carolina** and **West Virginia.**

Challenges of Families in the 1990s

Families today face unprecedented challenges in raising their youngsters. For many, the primary concerns are economic: nearly a third of all American workers earn wages that do not lift them out of poverty, even if they work full time.[1] Families with young children are particu-

> Traditional service systems focus on crisis intervention and strict eligibility requirements. Family support programs, by contrast, attempt to address family needs holistically. They build on families' strengths by helping parents improve their capacity to be supportive and nurturing and to cope with day-to-day stresses.

larly hard-hit economically: by 1990 those with children under three constituted the single largest group living in poverty. A quarter of such families fall below the poverty line, and poverty rates are even higher for African-American, Hispanic, and single-parent families with young children. In addition, real wages for younger, less experienced workers have declined disproportionately, with an even greater deterioration among less educated workers.[2] The decrease in the economic status of young parents is of particular concern because young children are especially vulnerable to family stress.

Many young parents resort to extraordinary measures to make ends meet and to arrange their child care. Among young parents working full time, close to half have at least one parent working outside regular daytime hours. Young parents often stagger their work schedules to avoid the costs of child care. But studies of "second-shift" families themselves report significant strains on the workers' marriages.[3]

Parents who turn to outside child care are concerned about the quality of care, particularly for very young children, and research confirms their fears. A 1992 study of 414 children in child care centers showed that 70 percent of infants and 52 percent of toddlers were in situations rated inadequate or barely adequate.[4] A 1994 study of family child care homes revealed that most of the homes in the study were rated as providing "custodial" care, only 9 percent were rated as providing care that enhanced children's development, and more than a third were rated inadequate.[5] In addition, the National Child Care Staffing Study found that the "quality of services provided by most centers was rated as 'barely adequate.'"[6]

Concern about balancing work and family life is not confined to those with the lowest incomes. Fully half the population report that they have too little time for their families. According to one study, most Americans of all incomes are actually working more hours than they did 20 years ago. In *The Overworked American,* author Juliet B. Schor reports that the average employee is working the equivalent of an extra month annually, because of both longer hours and more work weeks. And economist Victor Fuchs writes that the time parents have to spend with their children fell by 10 hours and 12 hours weekly for whites and blacks, respectively, between 1960 and 1986.[7]

Few workplaces offer "family-friendly" policies to help parents balance work and family responsibilities. The federal Family and Medical Leave Act, passed in 1993, offers some assistance, but 50 percent to 60 percent of workers are excluded from its coverage.[8] Furthermore, many new parents cannot afford to take the unpaid leave guaranteed under the act.

Problems of the Most Vulnerable Families

Although many families are able to sustain a nurturing family life despite their difficulties in making ends meet, some face almost insurmountable obstacles. Many indicators of child and family health declined during the last decade.

- Today, almost one quarter of children are being raised by one parent, most often a divorced or never-married mother.

- One in five children live in poor families, and the poverty rates among young families have nearly doubled in the last two decades.

- Half a million babies are born annually to teenagers who have little hope for a secure economic future.

- Drugs and violence are ravaging an increasing number of communities.

- Nearly 8.5 million children are currently without health insurance, even though two-thirds of these uninsured children have at least one parent who works full time.[9]

- An estimated 3.1 million children were reported abused or neglected

QUALITY IS IMPORTANT BUT HARD TO FIND

According to the Children's Defense Fund, too many children are in child care that does not meet their health, safety and developmental needs. Good quality care is not cheap, and poor children are the least likely to be in good-quality child care programs, despite the fact that their families are spending the highest proportion of their incomes for child care. Parents are deeply concerned about the quality of care their children receive: 97 percent of parents surveyed in a 1989 Harris poll cited quality as a top priority in child care.

—Gina Adams,
Children's Defense Fund
Who Knows How Safe?

in 1995, more than twice the number reported in 1980.[10] The number of children placed in foster care has increased 65 percent between 1984 and 1993 to an estimated 445,000 children.[11] Although poverty does not necessarily translate into abuse or neglect, analysis suggests that, among risk factors, poverty alone is consistently related to all categories of abuse and neglect.[12]

FAMILIES UNDER STRESS

Children need strong, stable families and enduring, supportive relationships. But as author Lisbeth Schorr observed in *Within Our Reach*, in families experiencing severe stress, love often turns into neglect, affection withers into hostility and discipline becomes abuse. Poverty, single parenthood, mental illness, drug abuse and social isolation can weaken families and impair some parents' ability to care for their children. When families are in turmoil, children are often the helpless victims of their parents' frustration and despair. In the absence of adequate support and services, these children are frequently removed from their families and placed in the custody of the state.

Clearly, families facing multiple stresses—including severe economic ones—are too often stretched beyond their capacities to cope. Public interventions frequently are the last resort, focusing on crisis services that are sometimes duplicative and expensive and often unable to ameliorate the problems that precipitated the family crisis in the first place.

Families and Government Programs: Diagnosing System Problems

As the problems faced by families have changed considerably over the past 20 years, public sector systems have been unable to keep pace. State legislatures have become concerned about the failure of service systems to address juvenile violence, child abuse and neglect, academic failure, childhood poverty and other social problems that threaten not only children and their families but the country's economic future. At the same time, state costs for

child welfare, mental health, juvenile justice, welfare, education and other social services continue to escalate.

State legislators are recognizing that the complex and uncoordinated array of services they have created to address specific symptoms, rather than the range of family needs, are in fact a major part of the system failure. Traditional service systems tend to proliferate services that are mandated—often the most costly—regardless of families' real needs. In addition, the increasing demand for such mandated services, coupled with state fiscal constraints, has prevented states from assisting families before their problems become acute, escalating into crises and demanding the most intrusive and expensive government intervention.[13] Many of the existing programs are so specialized that families who fail to meet narrow eligibility criteria fall through the cracks, while others end up with multiple caseworkers with little coordination among them.

Furthermore, federal poverty program expenditures have not kept pace with the increase in the numbers of poor families. The new federalism of the 1980s left states and localities with a greater degree of responsibility for social services but fewer federal resources to pay for them. Although state policymakers welcome the recognition of their roles as social welfare policy innovators under the 1996 federal welfare law, concerns exist about the adequacy of federal

SOCIAL PROBLEMS AND THE ECONOMY

In *Reinventing Systems: Collaborations to Support Families*, the Harvard Family Research Project describes the interrelationships among traditional service systems, social problems and economies: "Many key indicators of child and family health declined throughout the 1980s: federal, state and local budget cuts are putting a premium on the cost-effectiveness of services; and flagging local economies trigger increases in unemployment, homelessness and domestic violence. The situation has escalated in a vicious circle: deteriorating family circumstances necessitate an increase in costly interventions that, in turn, aggravate the economic perils of local economies. As a result, existing services are stretched thin, and families have an increasingly hard time getting the help they need."

funding in the long term especially when states face fiscal downturns.

Reinventing Services: Family Support Approaches

Because separate systems have not adequately addressed families' problems, policymakers are looking at multigenerational family support and education programs. In contrast to traditional services that focus on crisis intervention and strict eligibility requirements, family support programs attempt to address family needs holistically. Programs are designed to build on families' strengths—rather than responding to their deficits—by helping parents improve their capacity to be supportive and nurturing and to cope with day-to-day stresses. Programs often combine a specific emphasis on parent education and skill-building with better linkage to available public and private resources and a supportive network for families. These initiatives provide primary prevention services in an effort to avoid the need for more costly crisis intervention.

Family support programs vary in setting, format and emphasis. Some are neighborhood-based centers, some are school-linked or -based, some are home-visiting programs, some focus primarily on one outcome—like reducing the incidence of child abuse or teen pregnancy—and others have more broadly defined goals. Services provided by these programs include:

- information;
- parenting classes;
- feedback and guidance;
- joint problem-solving;
- direct advocacy and help with securing income security or other support services; and
- encouragement and emotional support.

This generic support is often combined with one or more concrete services needed by families, such as early care and education, respite care, job training, transportation, health or development screening, adult education and employment referral. All share a perspective on families that values and respects them and builds on their strengths. Consequently, specific services are flexible, focusing on family-defined needs and building families' own capacity to cope.

State legislatures across the country have funded a variety of early intervention, parent education and other types of family support services. Many programs have shown considerable promise in achieving specific outcomes, such as assisting parents in their familial roles, reducing the incidence of child abuse and neglect improving children's readiness for school and improving maternal and child health. The following are among the most well-known:

- **Hawaii**'s Healthy Start Program, which has documented success in child abuse prevention by targeting high-risk new mothers for home-visiting services;[14]
- **Maryland**'s Friends of the Family, a network of community-based family resource centers, which have

HOW FAMILY SUPPORT DIFFERS FROM TRADITIONAL SERVICES

Family Support Services	Traditional Services
Help prevent crises by meeting needs early	Intervene after crises occur and needs intensify
Offer help meeting basic needs, special services and referrals	Offer only specific services or treatments
Respond flexibly to family and community needs	Program and funding source dictate services
Focus on families	Focus on individuals
Build on family strengths	Emphasize family deficits
Reach out to families	Have strict eligibility requirements
Often offer drop-in services	Have rigid office hours
Respond quickly to needs	Often have waiting lists
Offer services in family's home or in home-like centers	Offer services in offices only

—Mary Lee Allen, Patricia Brown, and Belva Finlay
Helping Children by Strengthening Families

WHAT ARE SCHOOL-LINKED FAMILY SUPPORT SERVICES?

Located in or near schools, school-linked family support services provide students and families access to a mix of services and referrals, such as prenatal and child care for teen mothers, immunizations, health screenings, job training and referrals, substance abuse and mental health counseling, literacy, parenting courses, food and housing assistance, adult education, tutorial services, family planning, home-visiting and recreation. This array of services addresses problems that can interfere with student learning.

In a 1990 review of 20 evaluations of family support programs for low income families, project director Heather Weiss and co-author Robert Halpern of the Erikson Institute for Advanced Studies in Child Development found short-term improvements on one or more dimensions of maternal behavior in 68 percent of the studies. These included improvements in parent-child interaction, parent responsiveness and parents' understanding of how to stimulate children's development.

reduced repeat pregnancy rates and improved educational outcomes for participating teens;[15]

- **Missouri**'s Parents as Teachers program, which has had positive effects on children's school readiness and parent's child development knowledge, through its voluntary program of home visits by parent educators for families with children under age three;[16]
- **Iowa**'s Family Development and Self-Sufficiency Program, which provides ongoing intensive support and home visits for AFDC recipients who are at risk of long-term welfare dependency. A recent evaluation found that participants made improvement in education and training, employment, housing and family needs, and self-confidence, helping them reach self sufficiency;[17]
- **Kentucky**'s ambitious Family Resource and Youth Service Center Program for low-income elementary and high schools described in the box.

Because family support programs are relatively new, the research base for them still is being developed. But the evidence to date is promising. For more than a decade, the Harvard Family Research Project has assessed developments in the family support movement and noted the implications for policymakers.

KENTUCKY FAMILY SUPPORT PROGRAMS

The Kentucky Family Resource and Youth Service Center program was created by the legislature as part of the Kentucky Education Reform Act of 1990. Services are focused in or near schools in which at least 20 percent of the students are eligible for free lunches. The program is designed to reduce barriers to learning through school-based family support and parent involvement initiatives. In the 1992-93 school year, 18,912 families and 21,270 students were served. Health services and referrals are the most frequently used core services, but parent training, child care (both preschool and after school) and counseling services are also used extensively.[18] Several recent studies found that **Kentucky's** programs are successful in improving dropout rates, academic proficiency, parental participation, involvement of school officials, and connections with community agencies. A 1996 study conducted by the state school boards association found that dropout rates in high schools with family resource and youth service centers declined as compared to high schools without them. The study also found that schools with family resource centers or youth service centers had greater improvement in academic scores and attendance than did schools without centers.[19]

Another program is Kentucky Parent and Child Education (PACE). The PACE program addresses intergenerational illiteracy and the related problem of attracting industry to a state whose work force is undereducated. It began as an interest of House Education Committee Chair Roger Noe in 1985 and has expanded from a 12-district pilot program in to a statewide program funded at $3.6 million in 1990. PACE encompasses a preschool program for 3- and 4-year-olds based on the High/Scope curriculum model, and parent-child activities, literacy tutoring, adult basic education classes and GED coaching and parent support groups on personal, academic and vocational issues. PACE promotes positive attitudes toward academic achievement in both parents and children. The program is targeted to parents without a high school diploma or its equivalent and their 3- and 4-year-olds. The program has been discussed widely and adapted for use in other states.[20]

EARLY INTERVENTIONS PAY OFF

Research consistently shows that the earlier the intervention, the greater the success. For example, services provided for at-risk parents before abusive or neglectful behaviors develop result in a more positive and long-lasting effect on parent-child interactions. New parents also are more willing to voluntarily seek assistance and to interact with others in the community.

Family support services can:

- improve mother-infant bonding and maternal capacity to respond to the child's needs;

- increase the ability to care for the child's physical and developmental needs;

- reduce the number of unwanted pregnancies;

- increase the use of health care services and job training opportunities; lower welfare use; and

- increase high school completion rates and employment for the population served.

—Robert Halpern and Heather Weiss
Family Support and Education

Improvements also were reported in parents' awareness of their role as teachers and in the expectations they held for their children. In addition, research indicated the program's potential for reducing the incidence of child abuse and neglect. With regard to the program's effect on children, research has noted positive effects on infants' and young children's performance on developmental tests, although the authors noted that longitudinal research would be necessary to assess long-term effects.

Nonetheless, these assessments suggest the critical role of quality early childhood care and education in effective family support services. The authors concluded that "programs that combine parent support and direct developmental services to young children appear to hold the most promise of promoting improved long-term child development outcomes,

while not neglecting parents' own developmental and support needs."[21]

Institutional Barriers to Reform

Although many family support initiatives have shown great promise for achieving better outcomes for families, most are still modest in scale. Significant barriers exist to adoption of family support reforms across service delivery systems and to integration of early care and education services within broader reform efforts. State and federal funding structures continue to favor traditional service delivery, focusing primarily on crisis intervention. At worst, bureaucratic structures and special interests may resist significant changes; at best, well-meaning administrators, advocates and service providers disagree or are unsure how best to incorporate reform into institutional structures. In the field of early care and education alone, experts disagree about the most appropriate reform vehicle—public schools or separate community-based entities.

THE HIDDEN COSTS OF QUALITY CARE

The full costs of early care and education are often not apparent. Researchers are just beginning to learn the true costs, which are camouflaged by a number of hidden subsidies. A recent study of 401 child care centers found that more than 25 percent of the full cost of care and education was covered by some form of subsidy, primarily through low staff wages, building, rent or occupancy aid, volunteers, donated goods, and in-kind contributions. The majority of these hidden costs are borne by workers themselves through forgone wages and benefits. Since workers earn less than the average person with similar education and circumstances, the study's economic analysis concludes that workers in these centers are subsidizing as much as 19 percent of the centers' full costs. This may contribute to high turnover rates—43 percent and 58 percent for teachers and assistant teachers, respectively. When viewed from an economic perspective, parent fees only accounted for about half of the full cost of care.

Cost, Quality & Child Outcomes Study Team (1995) Cost, Quality and Child Outcomes in Child Care Centers, Public Report, April 1995, 2nd ed. (Denver: University of Colorado at Denver)

In addition, funding is scarce and short-term costs for reform can be even greater than continuing status quo service delivery arrangements because policymakers must continue to fund existing mandated services while phasing in new approaches. The short-term costs of quality early care and education per se are often not adequately addressed because early care programs are scattered throughout a hodge podge of separate systems under a variety of program auspices, regulatory structures and funding entities.

Legislative Barriers

Legislative institutions are also part of the problem. Some democratic legislative processes contribute to the inability to adequately respond to the real multifaceted needs of families. The procedural structures in state legislatures actually can preclude a holistic examination of overall state policy and response to vulnerable families.

The procedural orientation of state legislatures dictates the route that any issue follows, whether it involves a bill becoming a law or a program being reviewed for funding. The committee process is intended to facilitate the expert consideration of a huge number of matters that come before legislative bodies. Because it is virtually impossible for individual lawmakers to become experts on every bill, they rely on the committee process in which lawmakers develop particular expertise based on their committee assignments. Their colleagues rely on them to assure that each issue is addressed in detail by experts in committee before the bill is brought before the entire body for consideration.

TENNESSEE: A MODEL OF CROSS-JURISDICTIONAL COOPERATION

Tennessee's Joint Select Committee on Children and Youth, established in 1987, has been particularly effective in stimulating major reform and developing family supportive policies. As a select committee, its main responsibilities are to examine programs and services currently affecting children and families, to recommend legislation to the General Assembly's regular standing committees and to serve in a legislative oversight capacity to promote integrated policy and program development.

Several factors have contributed to the committee's effectiveness, but chief among them is participation by legislative leaders. The legislation creating the committee required participation by all relevant standing committees that review legislation affecting children and their families. Currently, the committee has 18 members, equally divided between the House and Senate. The members are lawmakers representing the Health and Human Resources, Judiciary, Education, Finance and Ways and Means committees. This representation across jurisdictions that also includes leaders ensures that the committee's work represents all perspectives and minimizes turf battles between existing standing committees. In **Tennessee**, the leadership views the committee as a helpful resource for accomplishing the goals of the standing committees, largely because leaders help shape the committee agenda.

The select committee serves as a unique vehicle for members to develop policy through in-depth, cross-jurisdictional study of family policies. Monthly interim meetings are scheduled for two-day periods to allow sufficient time to consider all relevant issues. Meetings often include site visits to state programs, as well as presentations by state and national program and policy experts. The committee's smooth functioning also is attributed to its strong, expert staffing. The current executive director has been with the committee since its inception in 1987 and has extensive experience in child and family policy issues.

The committee's accomplishments are impressive. It has overseen

* major restructuring of financing children's services in the state;

* establishment of a state entitlement for family preservation services for all families with a child facing state custody;

* creation of family resource centers and school-based Teen Learning Centers;

* establishment and expansion of the Child Care Facilities Program; and

* expansion of early intervention services for young children with disabilities.

Most recently, the committee spearheaded a juvenile violence prevention package through the 1994 legislative process that incorporated early childhood and family support as an integral prevention strategy.[22] This act also required development of a funding and implementation plan to provide early childhood programs for all at-risk three- and four-year-olds.[23]

But this structure can result in a disjointed view of complex interrelated problems like those faced by today's families. Thus, legislation related to child care services to enable welfare recipients to work are routed through human services committees, while preschool programs focusing on school-readiness for low-income youngsters are most often considered in a separate education committee. Routine regulation may be addressed by either committee separately or an entirely different committee or process. Issues related to "family-friendly" workplaces are most often addressed by labor committees, while judiciary committees often consider issues related to abuse in child care settings. In some states, program appropriations are handled by a budget committee. Consequently, no one legislative committee has an overall sense of how the variety of services and program regulations relate to one another in the early care field, let alone the larger context of overall family support reform.

Still, some state lawmakers are recognizing the implications of early care and education within committee jurisdictions that traditionally have not handled such issues. Examples of initiatives that pushed an early care agenda within and beyond conventional jurisdictions have been discussed in previous chapters. They include **Oregon, Tennessee** and **Washington.** Often pushed by visionary legislative champions who took advantage of opportunities to move an early childhood care agenda beyond its traditional scope, most of these initiatives represent incremental approaches that focused on achieving limited objectives relevant to the committee's primary jurisdiction—expanding economic development, improving children's academic performance, reducing juvenile violence or reducing parental welfare dependency. These initiatives are important in laying the foundation for further more comprehensive, interjurisdictional policy approaches.

Some legislatures already have recognized that historical structures contribute to fragmented policy deliberation on children's and family issues. Many have recently created new structures to address children and family issues across jurisdictions. In the last decade, there has been a proliferation of specialized legislative mechanisms to deliberate children's and family issues, including those in **California, Connecticut, Kansas, Massachusetts, Missouri, New York, Oregon** and **Tennessee.** Currently, almost half the states have created

CROSS-COMMITTEE APPROACHES TO EARLY CHILDHOOD AND FAMILY SUPPORT PROGRAMS

Another strategy legislators use to pass early childhood measures as part of family support packages is to generate a bill in committees with several jurisdictions. This approach involves legislators and legislative staff with relevant perspectives and input. Two examples are **Vermont** and **Wisconsin**, which enacted early childhood family support legislation in 1994.

Vermont lawmakers passed a bill providing coordinated, individualized early education and support programs to the child and family, including home-visiting.[24] In the House, the bill was introduced in the Education Committee before going to the Health and Welfare Committee and then back to the Education Committee. In the Senate, the Health and Welfare Committee heard the bill. The bill sponsor is on neither committee, but does sit on the Senate Finance Committee.

Wisconsin legislators enacted a grant program that coordinates family support and outreach through early childhood family education centers.[25] The bill was heard in the Senate Health, Human Services and Aging Committee and in the Assembly Health Committee, rather than the Assembly Children and Human Services Committee. As in Vermont, neither the Senate nor the Assembly bill sponsors sit on these committees. However, the Senate sponsor is a member of the Joint Finance Committee and the Assembly sponsor chairs the Financial Institutions Committee and sits on the Education Committee.

such structures. The type, duration and structure of each legislative committee varies by state. Also, there are 18 permanent standing committees, and at least 10 additional states have created other cross-jurisdictional legislative structures in an effort to coordinate policymaking on children and family issues.

State Legislative Initiatives: Family Support

To better address the needs of families, some legislatures are initiating major efforts to reform state service delivery

NORTH CAROLINA'S SMART START

"The **North Carolina** General Assembly finds, upon consultation with the governor, that every child can benefit from, and should have access to, high-quality early childhood and development services. The economic future and well-being of the state depend upon it. To ensure that all children have access to quality early childhood education and development services, the General Assembly further finds that:

1) Parents have the primary duty to raise, educate, and transmit values to young preschool children:

2) The state can assist parents in their role as the primary caregivers and educators of young preschool children; and

3) There is a need to explore innovative approaches and strategies for aiding parents and families in the education and development of young preschool children."

—1993 N.C. Sess. Laws, Chap. 321, Sec. 254

systems using family support models. This book highlights legislative efforts in **North Carolina** and **West Virginia** since these states' family support efforts integrate early care and education services as an integral component of the reform initiatives.

North Carolina: Smart Start

North Carolina's Smart Start is a comprehensive initiative designed to provide every child in the state access to affordable quality child care and early education and other crucial family support services. Approved in 1993, the legislative package included provisions and funding to upgrade the quality of existing early childhood services in the state and authorized the Smart Start program. Governor Hunt's leadership in proposing the Smart Start initiative was bolstered by a legislative constituency that had been proactive on child care issues for some time. Throughout the legislature's two-year interim study on child care, legislative advocates were educating their colleagues on needed reforms and were well-prepared not only to move the Smart Start agenda, but to enhance it.

This study committee proposed nine significant child care policy changes to the legislature in 1993. Some of these recommendations were enacted in Smart Start. They included increased child care appropriations to counties, expanded eligibility for child care assistance and better staff/child ratios for infants and toddlers in child

care. A study committee, under the auspices of the Legislative Research Commission, was headed by Representative Ruth Easterling, Senator James Richardson, Senator Russell Walker and Representative Howard Hunter, all of whom are appropriations committee members and longtime leading supporters of early childhood services.[26] Thus, the 1993 General Assembly made significant headway in establishing institutional mechanisms for a universal system of community-based family supports that incorporates quality early care and education services.

Smart Start has several key components:

1. Creation of the North Carolina Partnership for Children, a nonprofit, cross-agency, public/private partnership to implement a comprehensive state blueprint for improving early childhood, health and other family support services.

2. Establishment of a framework for local partnerships to demonstrate innovative systems of early childhood service delivery that meet the unique needs of communities.[27]

3. Since 1993-94, the program has expanded from 12 demonstration projects to 47 local partnerships that serve 55 counties. In 1996-97, the legislature appropriated $62.5 million for 35 existing local partnerships and $1.2 million for planning grants to 12 new partnerships ($100,000 each). The partnerships have considerable flexibility to fashion creative programs to meet the unique needs of families in their communities. Local partnerships also receive around $100,000 each (or 5 percent of their total allocation) for administration.[28]

4. More than $12.5 million for 1995-96 in teacher education and support, health initiatives, and community outreach and awareness.[29] Teacher support includes professional development for providers and incentives under the TEACH (Training, Education and Compensation Helps) program in the form of higher wages for providers who obtain more training credentials. Health initiatives include a health resource van, screenings, and outreach nurses.[30]

5. Delineation of a core set of early childhood services and program quality enhancements that may be provided by the local partnerships with new state funds. In 1994, the legislature expanded the list to include other direct services. These include supplements to reduce county waiting lists for subsidized care, resource and referral services, Head Start and local child care needs assessments. Partnerships also may use funds to increase child care reimbursement rates, raise the income eligibility ceiling for child care, and create incentives to reduce early childhood staff turnover.[31]

6. Each local partnership must use at least 30 percent of its direct service money toward child care subsidies, unless the county does not need that amount.[32]

The Smart Start program targets young families with children from birth to age five to ensure their healthy development and readiness for school. Through the local partnerships, participating counties have implemented a wide range of programs.[33] One county eliminated the waiting list for state subsidies, affecting 220 families. In other counties, child care workers are receiving better pay after completing credentials in early childhood education. Several counties are providing transportation through a new state/federal/county partnership in which a county can use Smart Start dollars and pay only 15 percent to 20 percent toward the cost of a van.[34] The state Department of Transportation finances the remainder using federal and state money.

In addition to $57.2 million in direct services, the legislature appropriated $10.2 million for 1996-97 for administration, planning and such state-level services as automation and evaluation.[35] Previous evaluation dollars funded a 1996 performance audit by Coopers and Lybrand, which recommended substantially increasing Smart Start funding. Accordingly, the legislature appropriated $67.4 million, more than tripling the amount appropriated for the program's first year in 1993. Even at this funding level, Smart Start covers just over half of the counties. In a legislatively mandated estimate, the Department of Human Resources projected the cost of fully funding Smart Start over the next five years to be $320 million.[36]

The performance audit concluded that "Smart Start is a credible program that delivers substantial good to children and families in the state of North Carolina." It is a highly innovative early childhood and health initiative that

has been very successful in bringing about county collaboration and new ways of delivering services.[37]

West Virginia: The Governor's Cabinet on Children and Families

Recognizing the need to coordinate early childhood programs, the **West Virginia** legislature created the Governor's Cabinet on Children and Families in 1990. To facilitate family support reforms, legislators authorized the independent cabinet to "nurture a flexible system for the comprehensive, unified, effective and efficient administration of programs and services to children and families which avoids fragmentation and duplication of programs and services and which facilitates and promotes cooperation among state agencies, as well as regional, local and private service agencies."[38]

The legislation authorized specific cabinet activities, some based on successful models, including parent education and home-based preschool instruction. Its wide-ranging goals include child care and development, housing, education, health and mental health services, job training and employment, nutrition, child protection, transportation, family literacy, substance abuse counseling and treatment and adolescent pregnancy prevention. The law authorizes the cabinet to coordinate children and family services by negotiating interagency agreements, developing early childhood standards and establishing local family resource networks that promote efficient service delivery. Two legislators, one from each chamber, and other academic and government officials serve as advisors to the cabinet.

As stated in the law, the cabinet is the focal point for local cross-agency initiatives. The cabinet works with the statutorily authorized local family resource networks to develop a community plan to improve services for children and families. The networks exist in 53 of the state's 55 counties. Drawing from a $1.4 million state-federal Family Resource Planning Fund, networks in 37 counties received money for planning coordination. This fund, a combination of a number of federal, state, and private funding streams, is expected to grow to more than $2 million in FY 1997.[39] An additional 15 counties receive "mini grants," mostly through the federal Family Preservation and Support Act. All counties receive state technical assistance, including the three without networks.[40]

In its six-year tenure, the cabinet has made early childhood services one of its top priorities. To further this priority, the governor created the cabinet's Early Child-hood Implementation Commission in April 1992.[41] A year later, the commission set forth the Action to Benefit Children (ABC) plan consisting of 16 recommendations that cover four major early childhood areas: (1) public awareness; (2) coordinated, comprehensive services; (3) family empowerment; and (4) staff training.

Local networks also can establish an early child-hood action plan. The state helps networks implement local plans by reconfiguring the service delivery system, that is, by adapting federal or state laws and regulations and funding streams to help implement local priorities.[42] Examples of local network action plan goals include (1) expansion of child care and parent education (2) smooth transitions of children with special needs from one program to another, and (3) cross-program training.[43]

The work of the Early Childhood Implemenation Commission has attracted additional private sector support. The AT&T Foundation awarded the commission an Early Education Quality Improvement Project (EQUIP) grant, coordinated by the New York City-based Families and Work Institute. The commission's initial work through the grant has been administration of parent and provider surveys on quality to assess current conditions and development and implementation of state and local quality improvement plans.[44] The Carnegie Corporation of New York and the Benedum Foundation are providing financial support for seven neighborhood centers for young children and their families, which bring together multiple services in one location.[45]

The cabinet supports an interagency approach to family resource coordination. This process is designed to assist family members in developing a plan to meet their needs and help them access appropriate services. To simplify processes, several counties have used a common application form and the state is developing a computer-ized family assessment, intake and referral system. In 1997 the state plans to provide one-time grants of $10,000 to each of 22 family resource networks to implement the computerized system.[46]

A recently created state Families First Council helps implement programs, serving as a liaison between state agencies and communities. Council members include representatives of human services, health, education, mental health, employment, and housing programs. Council members focus on how to use various funds to strengthen families. The cabinet also acts as the focal

point for the federal Family Preservation and Support Act's five-year plan through a contract with the state child welfare agency.[47]

Through the joint support of the legislative and executive branches in **West Virginia**, the state has embarked on comprehensive reform that integrates early childhood care and education services. State officials are conducting an evaluation of the original seven family resource networks by interviewing consumers and providers about their satisfaction with services and accessibility. The results will be ready in 1997.[48] Although evaluation data are not yet available, the initiative holds the potential to serve as a national model in incorporating early childhood policies and programs in a large family support reform effort.

Conclusion

In theory, at least, policymakers of all stripes profess the importance of the family. Few would argue with the words of the Family Resource Coalition:

The influence of the family on a child cannot be overestimated. The family is a child's first source of information and the primary model for how a child experiences relationships. It helps a child begin to communicate and to learn personal and cultural values and beliefs. The family teaches a child ways to live in a complex world, and it provides a child with a sense of belonging and a foundation for self-esteem. Families, and specifically parents, who are confident and effective in these responsibilities are more likely to raise healthy and productive children.[49]

As this chapter has shown, however, considerable stresses are weighing on many families today, hampering some in fulfilling their parental roles and resulting in bad outcomes for children. But as also illustrated, families are not hopeless, and the prognosis for even the most vulnerable can be changed with appropriate and high-quality support, including early childhood care and education services. Family issues are becoming main-stream on state political agendas as legislative leaders and other champions experiment with innovative family policies. Though many innovations are small in scale, they are nonetheless promising, and their outcomes and experiences will shape and inform tomorrow's policy agenda for children and families.

APPENDIX:
RESOURCES FOR FURTHER INFORMATION

List of National Early Childhood Organizations

Center for Career Development in Early Care and Education
Wheelock College
200 The Riverway
Boston, MA 02215
(617) 734-5200, ext. 211
Andrea Genser, Azra Farrell

Center for Law and Social Policy (CLASP)
1616 P Street, N.W.
Suite 450
Washington, DC 20036
(202) 328-5140
Mark Greenberg

Child Care Action Campaign (CCAC)
330 Seventh Avenue, 17th Floor
New York, NY 10032
(212) 239-0138
Barbara Reisman, Gail Richardson

Child Care Law Center (CCLC)
22 Second Street, 5th Floor
San Francisco, CA 94105
(415) 495-5498
Jo Ann Gong

Children's Defense Fund (CDF)
25 E Street, N.W.
Washington, DC 20001
(202) 628-8787
Gina Adams, Helen Blank

Children's Foundation
725 15th Street, N.W.
Suite 505
Washington, DC 20005-2109
(202) 347-3300
Sandy Gellert

Council of Chief State School Officers (CCSSO)
One Massachusetts Avenue, N.W.
Suite 700
Washington, DC 20001-1431
(202) 336-7033
Lynson Moore Bobo

Families and Work Institute
330 Seventh Avenue, 14th Floor
New York, NY 10001
(212) 465-2044
Ellen Galinsky, Robin Hardman

High/Scope Educational Research Foundation
600 North River Street
Ypsilanti, MI 48198
(313) 485-2000
Larry Schweinhart

National Association for Child Care Resource and Referral Agencies (NACCRRA)
1391 F Street, N.W.
Suite 810
Washington, DC 20004-1106
(202) 393-5501
Yasmina Vinci, Sarah Nordmann

National Association for the Education of Young Children (NAEYC)
1509 16th Street, N.W.
Washington, DC 20036-1426
(202)232-8777
Barbara Willer

National Center for Children in Poverty
Columbia University School of Public Health
154 Haven Avenue
New York, NY 10032
(212) 927-8793
Jane Knitzer, Stephen Page

National Center for the Early Childhood Work Force (NCECW)
733 15th Street, N.W., Suite 103
Washington, DC 20005
(202) 737-7700
Kendra Wright

National Conference of State Legislatures (NCSL)
1560 Broadway, Suite 700
Denver, CO 80202
(303) 830-2200
Scott Groginsky, Shelley Smith

National Economic Development and Law Center
2201 Broadway, Suite 815
Oakland, CA 94612-3024
(510) 251-2600
Janette E. Stokley

National Governors' Association (NGA)
444 North Capitol Street, N.W., Suite 250
Washington, DC 20001
(202) 624-5300
Susan Golonka

School-Age Child Care Project
Center for Research on Women
Wellesley College
106 Central Street
Wellesley, MA 02181-8259
(617) 283-2547
Michelle Seligson

Zero to Three
National Center for Infants, Toddlers and Families
2000 14th Sreet, North, Suite 380
Arlington, VA 22201-2500
(703) 528-4300
Beverly Jackson, Abbey Griffin

List of State Contacts

ECONOMIC

Maine
Barbara Collier
Maine Department of Human Services
Statehouse Station #11
Augusta, ME 04333
(207) 289-5060

Oregon
Dell Ford, Anita McClanahan
Oregon Department of Education
Oregon Head Start Collaboration Project
Office of Student Services
700 Pringle Parkway, S.E.
Salem, OR 97310-0290
(503) 378-5585

Washington
Mary Frost
Washington Department of Community, Trade and
Economic Development
906 Columbia Street, S.W.
P.O. Box 48300
Olympia, WA 98504-8300
(360) 586-1557

EDUCATION

Georgia
Brenda Hayes
Office of School Readiness
10 Park Place South, Suite 200
Atlanta, GA 30303
(404) 656-5957

Hawaii
Karen Hosaka
Hawaii Department of Education
P.O. Box 2360
Honolulu, HI 96804
(808) 735-9088

Kentucky
Debbie Schumacher
Kentucky Department of Education
Division of Early Childhood
500 Mero Street
Frankfort, KY 40601
(502) 564-7056

Ohio
Mary Lou Rush
Ohio Department of Education
Division of Early Childhood Education
65 South Front Street, Room 309
Columbus, OH 43266-0308
(614) 466-0224

FAMILY SUPPORT

North Carolina
Mary Ellen Sylvester
Legislative Fiscal Research Division
North Carolina General Assembly
Legislative Office Bldg., Room 619
Raleigh, NC 27603-5925
(919) 733-4910

West Virginia
Steve Heasley, Barbara Merrill
West Virginia Cabinet on Children and Families
Building 1, Room 9
1900 Kanawah Blvd., East
Charleston, WV 25305
(304) 558-0600

HEALTH

Arkansas
Glenda Bean
Arkansas Early Childhood Commission
101 East Capitol, Suite 106
Little Rock, AR 72201
(501) 682-4891

Indiana
Karen Priest
Indiana Family and Social Services Administration
W341 Indiana Government Center South
402 West Washington Street
Indianapolis, IN 46204-2739
(317) 232-1145

JUVENILE JUSTICE

North Carolina
Nadine Cook
North Carolina Department of Human Resources
Division of Child Development
319 Chaponake Road
Raleigh, NC 27613
(919) 662-4554

Joseph Canty
Support Our Students
3800 Barrett Drive, Suite 303
Raleigh, NC 27609
(919) 571-4848

Norman Camp
North Carolina Department of Public Instruction
Division of Instructional and Accountability Services
Education Building
301 N. Wilmington St.
Raleigh, NC 27601-2825
(919) 715-1504

Tennessee
(Position Vacant)
Joint Select Committee on Children and Youth
3rd Floor, James K. Polk Bldg.
Nashville, TN 37243-0061
(615) 741-6239

Washington
Susan Lucas
Washington Senate Ways and Means Committee
300 John A Cherberg Bldg., QW-12
Olympia, WA 98504
(360) 786-7711

WELFARE REFORM

Illinois
Michele Piel
Illinois Department of Public Aid
Division of Family Support Services
Child Care and Development Section
624 S. Michigan, 2nd Floor
Chicago, IL 60605
(312) 793-3610

Iowa
Don Kassar
Iowa Department of Human Services
Hoover Bldg.
Des Moines, IA 50319-0114
(515) 281-3186

Utah
Cathie Pappas
Utah Department of Human Services
Office of Family Support
120 North 200 West
Salt Lake City, UT 84103
(801) 538-3976

NOTES

Chapter 1

1. Forthcoming data from the Children's Defense Fund.

2. Gwen Morgan et al., *Making a Career of It* (Boston, Mass.: Wheelock College, Center for Career Development in Early Care and Education, 1993), 10.

3. The definitions of the Head Start, state prekindergarten programs and child care subsidy programs, and the discussion of barriers to collaboration rely heavily on unpublished material provided to the authors by Louise Stoney, Stoney Associates, Albany, N.Y., and from Gina Adams and Jodi Sandfort, *First Steps, Promising Futures: State Prekindergarten Initiatives in the Early 1990s* (Washington, D.C.: Children's Defense Fund).

4. Anne Mitchell, Heather Weiss, and Tom Schultz, *Evaluating Education Reform: Early Childhood Education*, paper prepared for the Office of Educational Research and Improvement, U.S. Department of Education, 1992, 2.

5. Lawrence J. Schweinhart, Helen V. Barnes, and David P. Weikart, *Significant Benefits: The High/Scope Perry Preschool Study Through Age 27* (Ypsilanti, Mich.: High/Scope Press, 1993), xix.

6. Ibid., 229.

7. Ibid.

8. Mitchell, Weiss, and Schultz, *Evaluating Education Reform*, 5-6.

9. Schweinhart, Barnes, and Weikart., *Significant Benefits*, 16.

10. Mitchell, Weiss, and Schultz, *Evaluating Education Reform*, 27.

11. Cost, Quality and Child Outcomes Study Team, *Cost, Quality and Child Outcomes in Child Care Centers, Public Report*, 2nd ed. (Denver: University of Colorado at Denver, 1995), 29, 35.

12. R. Ruopp, J. Travers, F. Glantz, & C. Coelen, *Children at the Center: Summary Findings and Their Implications*. Final Report of the National Day Care Study, vol. I (Cambridge, Mass.: Abt Associates, 1979).

13. Carnegie Task Force on Meeting the Needs of Young Children, *Starting Points: Meeting the Needs of Our Youngest Children* (New York, N.Y.: The Carnegie Corporation of New York, April 1994), 49.

14. National Center for the Early Childhood Work Force, *Child Care Staff Profile* (Washington, D.C.: NCECW, 1995).

15. National Association for the Education of Young Children, *Accreditation Criteria and Procedures,* Position Statement of the National Academy of Early Childhood Programs, Revised Edition-1991 (Washington, D.C.: NAEYC, 1991).

Chapter 2

1. NBC *Today Show*, February 2, 1994, (transcript of interview with authors Anne Weisberg and Carol Buckler), 15.

2. U.S. Department of Labor, Bureau of Labor Statistics, Current Population Survey Unpublished Tables, March 1996.

3. Mary Hawkins, U.S. Bureau of the Census, October 9, 1996: telephone conversation.

4. Lynne Casper, *How Much Does It Cost to Mind Our Preschoolers,* U.S. Census Bureau, Washington, D.C., publication P70-52, September 1995, 4.

5. Carnegie Task Force, *Starting Points*, 56.

6. Ibid.

7. U.S. Department of Labor, Bureau of Labor Statistics, *Employment and Earnings Annual Average*, Table 11, January 1996 ed.

8. Alice Burton, National Center for the Early Childhood Work Force, May 6, 1994: telephone conversation.

9. National Center for the Early Childhood Work Force, *Child Care Staff Profile* (Washington, D.C.: NCECW, 1995).

10. Catherine Sonnier, "Public/Private Partnerships in Child Care," *State Legislative Report* (National Conference of State Legislatures) 13, no. 33 (October 1988).

11. Whitebook, Phillips, and Howe, *National Child Care Staffing Study Revisited*, 7-8; U.S. House Committee on Ways and Means, *Overview on Entitlement Programs*, 1994 Green Book (Washington, D.C., July 15, 1994), 1155.

12. National Center for the Early Childhood Work Force, *Data Update, Child Care Teaching Staff Wage Trends* (Washington, D.C.: NCECW, November 1995).

13. Whitebook, Phillips, and Howe, *The National Child Care Staffing Study Revisited*, 7-9.

14. Ibid, 10.

15. R.H. McKey et al., *The Impact of Head Start on Children, Families and Communities: Head Start Synthesis Project. 85-31193*, (Washington D.C.: U.S. Department of Health and Human Services, 1985); M. Therese Gnezda and Shelley L. Smith, *Child Care and Early Childhood Education Policy: A Legislator's Guide* (Denver, Colo.: National Conference of State Legislatures, March 1989), 38.

16. Committee for Economic Development, *Investing In Our Children*, A statement by the Research and Policy Committee of the Committee for Economic Development (New York, N.Y.: CED 1985); Gnezda and Smith, *Child Care and Early Childhood Education Policy*, 38.

17. J. R. Berrueta-Clement et al. *Changed Lives: The Effects of the Perry Preschool Program on Youths Through Age 19* (Ypsilanti, Mich.: High/Scope Press, 1984); I. Lazar and R. Darlington, *Lasting Effects of Early Education: A Report from the Consortium for Longitudinal Studies*, Monograph Society for Research in Child Development, Serial No. 95. 4F (2-3), 1982; Gnezda and Smith, *Child Care and Early Childhood Education Policy*, 38.

18. Lawrence J. Schweinhart et al., *Significant Benefits*, xv.

19. Ray Marshall and Marc Tucker, *Thinking for a Living: Education and the Wealth of Nations* (New York, N.Y.: BasicBooks, 1992); Commission on the Skills of the American Work Force, *America's Choice: High Skills or Low Wages*, (Rochester, N.Y.: National Center on Education and the Economy, June 1990).

20. Committee for Economic Development, *Children In Need*, (New York, N.Y.: CED 1987).

21. Dan Pilcher, *Reorganizing Firms: Learning to Compete* (Denver, Colo.: National Conference of State Legislatures, forthcoming).

22. David Shreve and Scott Liddell, "Reading, Writing and Job Training," *State Legislatures* 17, no. 11 (November 1991): 33.

23. Secretary's Commission on Achieving Necessary Skills, *What Work Requires of Schools* (Washington, D.C.: U.S. Department of Labor, June 1991).

24. Marshall and Tucker, *Thinking for a Living*, xi.

25. Ibid.

26. Oregon Progress Board, *Human Investment Partnership: Achieving Benchmarks for Exceptional People* (Salem, Ore.: Oregon Progress Board, November 1991).

27. Ibid., 20-21.

28. 1991 Or. Laws, Chap. 693, Sec. 19a.

29. Anita McClanahan, Oregon Department of Education, October 1, 1996: telephone conversation.

30. Ibid.

31. Oregon Progress Board, *Investment Partnership: Achieving Benchmarks for Exceptional People* (November 1991).

32. Anita McClanahan, Oregon Department of Education, October 1, 1996: telephone conversation.

33. Gnezda and Smith, *Child Care and Early Childhood Education Policy*, 56.

34. Ibid.

35. Mary Frost, Washington Department of Community Development, August 1994: telephone conversation.

36. Jennifer Priddy and Laura Walkush, *1992 ECEAP Longitudinal Study and Annual Report* (Olympia, Wash.: Washington Department of Community Development, 1993).

37. Gnezda and Smith, *Child Care and Early Childhood Education Policy*, 56.

38. Cathie Halpin, Washington Department of Community, Trade and Economic Development, October 15, 1996: telephone conversation.

39. Ibid.

40. Ibid.

41. U.S. General Accounting Office, *Employment Training: Successful Projects Share Common Strategy*, May 1996, 11.

42. U.S. General Accounting Office, *Child Care Subsidies Increase Likelihood That Low-Income Mothers Will Work*, December 1994, 7.

43. Ibid., 5.

44. Peter Cattan, "Child-Care Problems: An Obstacle to Work," *Monthly Labor Review* (October 1991): 3-9.

45. "Child Care Problems Force Workers To Quit," *Report on Preschool Programs*, February 10, 1993, 26.

46. "More Firms Offer Child Care Benefits," *Report on Preschool Programs*, August 26, 1992, 173.

47. "Child Care is Top Priority For Relocating Workers," *Report on Preschool Programs*, April 6, 1994, 65.

48. U.S. General Accounting Office, *Job Training Partnership Act: Actions Needed to Improve Participant Support Services* (Washington, D.C., June 1992).

49. Cynthia Ransom and Sandra Burud, *Productivity Impact Study of an On-site Child Care Center*, (Pasadena, Calif.: Burud and Associates, May 1989).

50. "Child Care Programs Emerge as Net Plus for Company," *Report on Preschool Programs*, October 20, 1993, 206.

51. "More Firms Offer Child Care Benefits," *Report on Preschool Programs*, August 26, 1992, 173.

52. Ibid.

53. Shelly Isaacson, Work/Family Directions, October 9, 1996: telephone conversation.

54. 1983 Md. Laws, Chap. 585.

55. Maryland Business and Economic Development Department, *Day Care Financing Highlights*, August 1996.

56. Sonnier, "Public/Private Partnerships in Child Care," 2.

57. Maryland Business and Economic Development Department, *Day Care Financing Highlights,* August 1996.

58. Joan Case, Maryland Business and Economic Development Department, October 10, 1996: telephone conversation.

59. 1989 Ark. Acts, Act 202; 1985 Cal. Stats., Chap. 1440; 1987 Conn. Acts, P.A. 435; 1989 Fla. Laws, Chap. 379; 1987 Me. Acts, Chap. 379; 1988 Md. Laws, Chap. 248; 1989 N.H. Laws, Chap. 411; 1994 N.Y. Laws, A.B. 12205; 1992 N.C. Sess. Laws, Chap. 900; 1989 Tenn. Pub. Acts, Chap. 420; 1989 Wash. Laws, Chap. 430.

60. 1987 R.I. Pub. Laws, Chap. 432.

61. 1988 Fla. Laws, Chap. 337.

62. 1990 Fla. Laws, Chap. 306.

63. "Creating New Child Care Slots: Big Bang for the Buck in New Jersey", *Children Today,* no. 1. (1992).

64. 1985 Fla. Laws, Chap. 118.

65. 1987 Or. Laws, Chap. 682.

66. 1993 Ark. Acts, Chap. 820.

67. Arizona Revised Statutes 43-1130; 1991 Cal. Stats., Chap. 476; 1990 Colo. Sess. Laws, Chap. 220; 1988 Conn. Acts, P.A. 289; 1992 Kan. Sess. Laws, Chap. 124; 1987 Me. Laws, Chap. 343; 1988 Md. Laws, Chap. 641; 1989 Miss. Laws, Chap. 524; 1989 Mont. Laws, Chap. 706; 1986 N.M. Laws, Chap. 20; 1982 Ohio Revised Code, Sec. 5709.65; 1985 Pa. Laws, Act 102; 1987 R.I. Pub. Laws, Chap. 477; 1988 S.C. Acts, Act 658.

68. Child Care Action Campaign, *Employer Tax Credits for Child Care: Asset or Liability?* (New York, N.Y.: Child Care Action Campaign, November 1989), v.

69. 1990 Mass. Acts, Chap. 521.

70. 1988 Wash. Laws, Chap. 236.

71. 1990 Cal. Stats., Chap. 181; 1990 Okla. Sess. Laws, Chap. 281; 1989 Tex. Gen. Laws, Chap. 1207; 1993 Wash. Laws, Chap. 194.

72. Sonnier, "Public/Private Partnerships in Child Care," 3.

73. The National Association of Child Care Resource and Referral Agencies, *NACCRRA Counts, 1994 State Administrators' Survey,* 38.

74. Representative Ed Pineau, Maine, September 15, 1994: telephone conversation.

75. U.S. Department of Labor, *The American Work Force: 1992-2005,* Bureau of Labor Statistics Bulletin 2452 (Washington, D.C., April 1994), 56, 64.

Chapter 3

1. Carnegie Task Force, *Starting Points,* 6-12.

2. Wanda Bailey, National Dropout Prevention Center, October 25, 1996: telephone conversation.

3. The National Dropout Prevention Center, Clemson University. *The Reality of Dropping Out* (Clemson, S.C.: 1995).

4. Carnegie Foundation for the Advancement of Teaching, "Ready to Learn: National Survey of Kindergarten Teachers"(New York, N.Y.: Carnegie Corporation of New York, 1991, photocopy).

5. Schweinhart, Barnes, and Weikart, *Significant Benefits,* 69.

6. Berrueta-Clement et al., *Changed Lives;* Lazar and Darlington, *Lasting Effects of Early Education;* Gnezda and Smith, *Child Care and Early Childhood Education Policy,* 38.

7. Berrueta-Clement, *Changed Lives;* Gnezda and Smith, *Child Care and Early Childhood Education Policy,* 38; Committee for Economic Development, *Investing In Our Children* (New York, N.Y.: CED, 1985).

8. Ibid.

9. Committee for Economic Development, *The Unfinished Agenda: A New Vision for Child Development and Education* (Washington, D.C.: CED, 1991), 28.

10. Schweinhart, Barnes, and Weikart, *Significant Benefits,* 154.

11. Gina Adams and Jodi Sandfort, *First Steps, Promising Futures: State Prekindergarten Initiatives in the Early 1990s* (Washington, D.C.: Children's Defense Fund, 1994).

12. U.S. General Accounting Office, *Poor Preschool-Aged Children: Numbers Increase but Most Not in Preschool* (Washington, D.C., July 1993), 2.

13. Ibid.

14. Adams and Sandfort, *First Steps.*

15. Ibid.

16. Vol. 69 Del. Laws, Chap. 351 (1994); 1992 Ga. Laws, 3173; 1993 N.C. Sess. Laws, Chap. 561, Part 22; 1995 Va. Acts, Chap. 852; 1996 Tenn. Pub. Acts., Chap. 954.

17. Debbie Schumacher, Kentucky Department of Education, August 17, 1994: telephone conversation.

18. "Key Elements of Kentucky Blended Classes" (Frankfort, Ky.: Department of Education, 1993); Debbie Schumacher, August 17, 1994: telephone conversation.

19. Debbie Schumacher, August 17, 1994 and October 11, 1996: telephone conversation.

20. Debbie Schumacher, October 11, 1996: telephone conversation.

21. Preschool Education Program Regulations for Four-Year-Old Children, 704 KAR 3:410.

22. Debbie Schumacher, August 17, 1994: telephone conversation.

23. *KERA Preschool 1990-93 Results* (Frankfort, Ky., Department of Education).

24. Jerry Scott, Ohio Department of Education, November 20, 1996: telephone conversation.

25. Ibid.

26. 1993 Ohio Laws, H.B. 152, Sec. 36.

27. Jerry Scott, telephone conversation.

28. Chris Stoneburner, Ohio CDF, August 17, 1994: telephone conversation.

29. Chris Stoneburner, September 28, 1994: telephone conversation.

30. Ohio Legislative Budget Office, Catalog of Special Purpose Accounts, Department of Human Services, 1995, 341.

31. Ohio Representative Charleta Tavares, October 18, 1996: telephone conversation.

32. Nancy DeRoberts Moore, Ohio Department of Education, October 21, 1996: telephone conversation.

33. Head Start Collaboration Project, *Child Care, Head Start and Education Partnerships Service Delivery Options* (Columbus: Ohio Department of Education, Division of Early Childhood Education, November 1995).

34. Elizabeth Levitan Spaid, "An All-Expense-Paid Pre-school Education," *Christian Science Monitor*, Aug. 29, 1996, 1.

35. Georgia State University, Department of Early Child-hood Education, Georgia Prekindergarten Evaluation (Atlanta: Georgia State University, September 1996) 1-2.

36. Spaid, "Paid Preschool Education."

37. 1996 Tenn. Pub. Acts, Chap. 954 and 1995 Va. Acts, Chap. 852, Sec. 22.1-199.1-C.

38. Jane Knitzer and Stephen Page, *Map and Track: State Initiatives for Young Children and Families* (New York, N.Y.: National Center for Children in Poverty, 1996), 33.

39. Brenda Hayes, Georgia Office of School Readiness, October 23, 1996: telephone conversation.

40. U.S. Department of Education, "National Study of Before- and After-School Programs," Final Report to the Office of Policy and Planning, U.S. Department of Education, Contract No. LC89051001, (Washington, D.C., 1993).

41. Michelle Seligson and Dale B. Fink, *No Time To Waste: An Action Agenda for School-Age Child Care* (Wellesley, Mass.: Wellesley College Center for Research on Women, 1989), 4.

42. Ibid., xii.

43. Seligson and Fink, *No Time To Waste*, xii.

44. U.S. Census Bureau, *Who's Minding the Kids? Child Care Arrangements: Fall 1991* (Washington, D.C.: U.S. Census Bureau, 1991), 1.

45. U.S. Census Bureau, *Who's Minding the Kids? Statistical Brief* (Washington, D.C.: U.S. Census Bureau, April 1994).

46. "Extension SACC Programs Support At-Risk Children," *Report on Preschool Programs* (January 25, 1995), 13.

47. Jill K. Posner and Deborah Lowe Vandell, "Low-Income Children's After-School Care: Are There Beneficial Effects of After-School Programs?" *Child Development 65* (1994): 454.

48. Deborah Lowe Vandell and Jill Posner, *Conceptualization and Measurement of Children's After-School Environments* (Madison: University of Wisconsin, March 27, 1996), 23.

49. Posner and Vandell, "Low-Income Children's After-School Care," 441.

50. Deborah Lowe Vandell, Lee Shumow, and Jill K. Posner, *Children's After-School Programs: Promoting Resiliency or Vulnerability?*, (Madison: University of Wisconsin, 1996), 39-40.

51. U.S. Census Bureau, *Who's Minding the Kids? Fall 1991*, 11.

52. U.S. Census Bureau, *Who's Minding the Kids? Statistical Brief*.

53. U.S. Department of Education, "National Study of Before- and After-School Programs," 15.

54. Ibid., 7.

55. Ibid., 111.

56. Anne Mitchell et al., *Early Childhood Programs and The Public Schools* (Dover, Mass.: Auburn House, 1989), 54.

57. Seligson and Fink, *No Time To Waste*, 34.

58. Ibid.

59. Colleen Mulligan, New York State School-Age Child Care Program, October 13, 1994: telephone conversation.

60. Seligson and Fink, *No Time To Waste*, 34. State funding was discontinued in the early 1990s. Programs are now funded by federal money. Barbara Collier, Maine Department of Human Services, September 13, 1994: telephone conversation.

61. 1990 Hawaii Sess. Laws, Act 334.

62. Linda Chung, Hawaii Department of Education, Office of Accountability and School Instructional Support, October 9, 1996: telephone conversation.

63. Clay Springer, Hawaii Senate Ways and Means Committee, October 8, 1996: telephone conversation.

64. 1990 Hawaii Sess. Laws, Act 334, Sec. 8.

65. Harumi Nishibun, September 13, 1994: telephone conversation.

66. Fern Marx and Michelle Seligson, *Interim Report on a Survey of the Hawaii After School (A+) Program* (Wellesley, Mass.: Wellesley College Center for Research on Women), May 1991, 24.

67. Diana Gardenhire, Indiana Family and Social Services Administration, May 20, 1994: telephone conversation; National Conference of State Legislatures, *State Legislative Summary: Children, Youth, and Family Issues* (Denver, Colo.: NCSL, 1991), 27.

68. Seligson and Fink, *No Time To Waste,* 34-35.

69. 1989 Tex. Gen. Laws, Chap. 1192.

70. National Conference of State Legislatures, *State Legislative Summary: Children, Youth, and Family Issues* (Denver, Colo.: NCSL, 1986-96).

71. 1991 Cal. Stats., Chap. 809.

72. U.S. General Accounting Office, *School-Linked Human Services A Comprehensive Strategy for Aiding Students at Risk of School Failure* (Washington, D.C., December 1993), 3.

73. Ibid., 1.

74. "Programs and Policies Aid Teen Parents and Their Children," news release (Wellesley, Mass.: Wellesley College Center Research on Women, August 1991).

75. Helen Blank, *Investing In Our Children's Care: An Analysis and Review of State Initiatives To Strengthen the Quality and Build the Supply of Child Care Funded Through the Child Care and Development Block Grant* (Washington, D.C.: Children's Defense Fund, June 1993), 15.

76. "Child Care Services Essential for Welfare Reform Programs," *Report on Preschool Programs,* September 8, 1993, 176.

77. U.S. General Accounting Office, *School-Linked Human Services,* 3-4.

78. Children's Defense Fund, *State Child Care Fact Book 1987* (Washington, D.C.: CDF, 1987), 41.

79. 1991 Or. Laws, Chap. 871.

80. 1990 Va. Acts, Chap. 939.

81. 1992 Iowa Acts, Chap. 1221.

82. The Center for the Study of Family, Neighborhood and Community Policy, *Welfare Reform: Impact on Public Education* (The University of Kansas, Lawrence, Kansas: November 6, 1996).

83. Catherine Sonnier, "Status of State Involvement," *State Legislative Report* 13, no. 16 (June 1988), 1.

Chapter 4

1. National Conference of State Legislatures, *State Legislative Summary: Children, Youth, and Family Issues* (Denver, Colo.: NCSL, 1995 and 1996).

2. American Psychological Association, *Violence and Youth: Psychology's Response, Vol. 1. Summary Report of the American Psychological Association Commission on Violence and Youth* (Washington, D.C.: American Psychological Association, 1993), 6-7.

3. Federal Bureau of Investigation, *Crime in the United States 1995.* (Washington D.C.: U.S. Department of Justice, October 1996).

4. Ibid.

5. Jones and Krisberg, *Images and Reality,* 2, 10.

6. Bart Lubow, Annie E. Casey Foundation, Presentation at NCSL's Annual Meeting, New Orleans, July 27, 1994.

7. Howard N. Snyder, Melissa Sickmund, and Eileen Poe-Yamagata, *Juvenile Offenders and Victims: 1996 Update on Violence* (Washington, D.C.: Office of Juvenile Justice and Delinquency Prevention, February 1996), 22.

8. Bart Lubow, Presentation at NCSL's Annual Meeting.

9. Snyder, Sickmund, and Poe-Yamagata, *Juvenile Offenders and Victims,* 24.

10. Corina Eckl, *State Budget Actions 1993* (Denver, Colo.: National Conference of State Legislatures, 1993), 22-23.

11. Ron Snell and Arturo Perez, *State Budget Actions 1996* (Denver, Colo: National Conference of State Legislatures, 1996), 24.

12. George M. and Camille Graham Camp, *The Corrections Yearbook 1994: Juvenile Corrections* (South Salem, N.Y.: Criminal Justice Institute, 1994), 35-36; George M. and Camille Graham Camp, *The Corrections Yearbook 1995: Juvenile Corrections,* (South Salem, N.Y.: Criminal Justice Institute, 1995), 35-36.

13. George M. and Camille Graham Camp, *The Corrections Yearbook 1995:* 37-38.

14. Jones and Krisberg, *Images and Reality,* 38-40.

15. Ibid. 5.

16. Elliott, *Youth Violence: An Overview,* 9.

17. Ibid.

18. Jones and Krisberg, *Images and Reality,* 4.

19. Donna Lyons, Mary Fairchild, and Shelley Smith, *A Legislator's Guide to Comprehensive Juvenile Justice* (Denver, CO: National Conference of State Legislatures, August, 1996).

20. Schweinhart, Barnes, and Weikart, *Significant Benefits,* 161-162.

21. Elliott, *Youth Violence: An Overview,* 2

22. Schweinhart, Barnes and Weikart, *Significant Benefits,* 83, 87; W. Steven Barnett, *The Perry Preschool Program and Its Long-Term Effects: A Benefits-Cost Analysis,* Hogh/Scope, no. 2, 1985, 41-42.

23. Schweinhart, Barnes, and Weikart, *Significant Benefits,* 83, 87.

24. Gregory J. McDonald, U.S. General Accounting Office, *Reducing Youth Violence: Coordinated Federal Efforts and Early Intervention Strategies Could Help,* report read as testimony before the U.S. Senate Committee on Governmental Affairs, March 31, 1992, 6.

25. Ibid.

26. Patricia J. Marzek and Robert J. Hagerty, "Reducing Risks for Mental Disorders: Frontiers for Prevention Intervention Research," *Illustrative Preventive Intervention Research Programs* (1994): 242-243.

27. David Hawkins, *Communities That Care, Risk Focused Prevention: What Does It Mean for Community Prevention Planning* (Seattle, Wash.: Developmental Research and Programs, Inc., 1993), 9.

28. David Huizinga et al., *Urban Delinquency and Substance Abuse, Initial Findings, Research Summary* (Washington, D.C.: Office of Juvenile Justice and Delinquency Prevention, March 1994), 15.

29. Eric Zorn, "People Who Are Criminals Have Very Little to Lose," *Daily Camera* (Boulder, Colo.), February 17, 1994, 1D.

30. Brenda J. Robinson, and Shelley L. Smith. "When Home's Not Sweet," *State Legislatures* (National Conference of State Legislatures) 21, no. 6 (June, 1995) 32-37.

31. Elliott, *Youth Violence: An Overview,* 3.

32. Cathy Spatz Widom, *The Cycle of Violence* (Washington, D.C.: National Institute of Justice, October 1992).

33. "Neuropsychiatric, Psychoeducational, and Family Characteristics of 14 Juveniles Condemned to Death in the United States," *American Journal of Psychiatry* 145.5 (May 1988): 588; Dorothy Otnow Lewis et al., "Toward a Theory of the Genesis of Violence: A Follow-up Study of Delinquents," *Journal of the American Academy of Child Adolescent Psychiatry* 28, no. 3 (1989): 431-436.

34. Schweinhart, Barnes and Weikart, *Significant Benefits,* 58-59.

35. David P. Weikart, *Quality Preschool Programs: A Long-Term Social Investment,* Occasional Paper No. 5, Ford Foundation Project on Social Welfare and the American Future (New York: Ford Foundation, June 1989), 6-7.

36. Schweinhart, Barnes, and Weikart, *Significant Benefits,* 97-98.

37. "Healthy Growth for Hawaii's 'Healthy Start': Toward a Systematic Statewide Approach to the Prevention of Child Abuse and Neglect," *Zero to Three*, April 1991, 20.

38. *Healthy Start*, Report to the Sixteenth Legislature 1992, Honolulu, Hawaii, 22.

39. Gregory J. McDonald, *Reducing Youth Violence*, 6.

40. Vol. 69 Del. Laws, H. 351, 1994.

41. Michael Morton, Delaware Comptroller General's Office, October 22, 1996: telephone conversation.

42. Section 67, Subdivision 4 of Minnesota's Omnibus Juvenile Justice Bill (HF 2074).

43. Carolyn Kampman, Colorado Joint Budget Committee, October 28, 29, 1996: telephone conversation

44. 1996 Colo. Sess. Laws, Chap. 84.

45. Kroshus, "Preventing Juvenile Violence."

46. *1994 Annual Report on Children's Initiatives*, Tennessee General Assembly, Select Committee on Children and Youth, June 9, 1994, 2, 6.

47. 1994 Tenn. Pub. Acts, Chaps. 802, 821 and 823.

48. "Juvenile Crime: Tennessee House OKs Bills on Juvenile Crime Prevention and Prevention," *Family Relations* 48, 16 (April 18, 1994).

49. 1994 N.C. Special Sess. Laws, Chap. 22.

50. 1994 N.C. Special Sess. Laws, Chap. 24.

51. Nadine Cook, North Carolina Department of Human Resources, Division of Child Development, October 22-23, 1996: telephone conversations.

52. 1994 N.C. Special Sess. Laws, Chap. 24, Sec. 31.

53. Barbara Farmer, North Carolina Department of Human Resources, October 3, 1994: telephone conversation.

54. Joseph Canty, Division of Youth Services, Department of Human Resources, Support Our Students program, October 23, 1996: telephone conversation.

55. *Intervention/Prevention Initiatives*, North Carolina General Assembly, 1993-1994 Session and Extra Session on Crime.

56. North Carolina Department of Human Resources, Office of the Secretary, *List of SOS Neighborhood Grants*, October 1994.

57. Norman Camp, Public Schools of North Carolina, Office of Instructional Services, November 15, 1996: telephone conversation; NC Sess. Laws, Chap. 24, Sec. 42-43.

58. Public Schools of North Carolina, Office of Instructional Services, *Consolidation of the Public School Fund Budget Beginning With 1995-96,* (Raleigh, N.C.: 1995).

59. Susan Lucas, Washington Senate Ways and Means Committee, October 22-23, 1996: telephone conversation.

60. 1994 Wash. Laws, Chap. 7, Secs. 305, 306, 604 First Special Session.

61. 1994 Wash. Laws, Chap. 7, Secs. 307, 308 First Special Sesssion.

62. Tim Yowell, October 4, 1994: telephone conversation.

63. Elliott, *Youth Violence: An Overview,* 2.

64. Jones and Krisberg, *Images and Reality,* 4.

65. "NGA Report Cites Risks, Strategies Aimed At Preventing Youth Violence," *Child Protection Report,* February 4, 1994, 22.

66. Ibid.

Chapter 5

1. Carnegie Task Force, *Starting Points,* 66-67.

2. Barbara Starfield, *Primary Care, Concept, Evaluation, and Policy* (Baltimore: Johns Hopkins University, Oxford University Press, 1992), 26, 38, 43; Anne S. Johansen et al., *Analysis of the Concept of Primary Care for Children and Adolescents: A Policy Research Brief* (Baltimore: Johns Hopkins University, 1994), 3.

3. Jack Elinson et al., *Outcome Evaluation of a Pediatric Health Care Model,* report prepared for the Maternal and Child Health Research Program (New York: Medical and Health Association of New York City, Inc., July 1993), 78-80.

4. "Cost Effectiveness of a Routine Varicella Vaccination Program for U.S. Children," *Journal of the American Medical Association* 271, no. 5 (February 2, 1994): 375.

5. Joel W. Hay and Robert S. Daum, "Cost-Benefit Analysis of Haemophilus Influenza Type b Prevention: Conjugate Vaccination at Eighteen Months of Age," *Pediatric Infectious Disease Journal* 9, no. 4 (April 1990): 246-252.

6. Martha King, *Saving Lives and Money: Preventing Low Birthweight* (Denver, Colo.: National Conference of State Legislatures, October 1988), 12.

7. Carnegie Task Force, *Starting Points*, 63.

8. Ibid., 43.

9. National Education Goals Panel, *The National Education Goals Report, Volume 1.* (Washington, D.C., 1993), 190 and 193.

10. Magda G. Peck and Harry Bullerdiek, "FAX Survey Reveals Strong Connections Between Urban Health Departments and Head Start," *cityData*, Fall 1993, 9.

11. Debra Hawks, American College of Obstetricians and Gynecologists, October 1994: written communication.

12. Southern Regional Project on Infant Mortality, *Countdown to 2000: Survey of State Action in Maternal and Child Health* (Washington, D.C.: Southern Regional Project, 1994), Vol. 2, 9.

13. Health Care Financing Administration, "Medicaid National Summary Statistics" (June 1996). URL=http://www.hcfa.gov, World Wide Web.

14. Linda Sizelove, U.S. Health Care Financing Administration, October 11, 1994: telephone conversation.

15. P.L. 103-66. Title IV-B of the Social Security Act, Subpart 2, The Family Preservation and Support Services; Omnibus Budget Reconciliation Act of 1993; 45 CFR, Part 92.

16. Association of Maternal and Child Health Programs, *Building on the Basics: Four Approaches to Enhancing MCH Service Delivery* (Washington, D.C.: AMCHP, December 1990), 6.

17. National Early Childhood Technical Assistance System, *Health Services for Young Children Under IDEA, paper no. 1* (Chapel Hill, N.C.: National Early Childhood Technical Assistance System, May 1994), 2-5; Catherine Sonnier, *Implementing Early Intervention Services for Infants and Toddlers with Disabilities* (Denver, Colo.: The National Conference of State Legislatures, 1990), 19.

18. Barbara Aliza, Association of Maternal and Child Health Programs, October 14, 1994: telephone conversation.

19. Children's Defense Fund, *Medicaid Reforms for Children: An EPSDT Chartbook* (Washington, D.C.: CDF, September 1992), 132-133.

20. National Commission on Children, *Increasing Educational Achievement: Implementation Guide Series*, (Washington, D.C.: National Commission on Children, 1993), 25-26.

21. Medicaid Bureau, Health Care Financing Administration, *EPSDT: A Guide for Educational Programs* (Washington, D.C.: U.S. Department of Health and Human Services, September 1992), 22.

22. Frank Farrow and Tom Joe, "Financing School-linked Integrated Services," *The Future of Children* (Center for Future of Children, The David and Lucille Packard Foundation) 2, no. 1 (Spring 1992), 56.

23. Suzanne Danilson, Louisiana Department of Health, September 21, 1994: telephone conversation.

24. 1991 Ind. Acts, P.L. 34, Sec. 21.

25. Karen Priest, *Indiana Family and Social Services Administration,* Step Ahead Program, October 18, 1996: telephone conversation.

26. "For Head Start Grantees Pitfalls of Working with Medicaid," *Day Care USA*, February 22, 1993, 5.

27. Head Start, "Head Start Collaboration Projects," (Washington, D.C.: U.S. Department of Health and Human Services [1994], photocopy).

28. Children's Defense Fund, *State of America's Children Yearbook* 1996, (Washington, D.C.: CDF, 1996), 22-23.

29. Martha King, *Healthy Kids* (Denver, Colo.: National Conference of State Legislatures, April 1993), 26.

30. National Conference of State Legislatures, *State Legislative Summary: Children, Youth, and Family Issues* (Denver, Colo.: NCSL, 1991-1995).

31. 1993 Kan. Sess. Laws, Chap. 89.

32. 1993 S.C. Acts, Act 35.

33. 1992 Cal. Stats., Chaps. 566 and 1320.

34. 1991 Minn. Laws, Chap. 569, Sec. 12.

35. Carnegie Task Force, *Starting Points*, xiii.

Chapter 6

1. Carnegie Task Force, *Starting Points*, 49.

2. Lawrence J. Schweinhart, *Quality of Care is Crucial to Young Children's Development*, testimony before the Subcommittee on Children, Family, Drugs and Alcoholism, House Committee on Labor and Human Resources, January 24, 1989.

3. Deborah Phillips et al., "The Social Policy Context of Child Care: Effects on Quality," *American Journal of Community Psychology 20 (1992)*: 25-51.

4. Barbara Willer, *Reaching the Full Cost of Quality in Early Childhood Programs* (Washington, D.C.: National Association for the Education of Young Children, 1990), 28

5. John M. Love, *Does Children's Behavior Reflect Day Care Classroom Quality?* (Princeton, N.J.: Mathematica Policy Research, 1993), 6.

6. Cost, Quality, and Child Outcomes Study Team, *Cost, Quality and Child Outcomes in Child Care Centers:* 2nd ed. (Denver: University of Colorado at Denver, 1995), 33.

7. Willer, *Reaching the Full Cost of Quality in Early Childhood Programs*, 28.

8. Ibid., 30.

9. Gina Adams, *Who Knows How Safe?* (Washington, D.C.: Children's Defense Fund, 1990), 112.

10. Ibid., 2.

11. Ellen Galinsky et al., *The Study of Children in Family Child Care and Relative Care: Highlights of Findings* (New York, N.Y.: Family and Work Institute, 1994), 4.

12. Gwen Morgan, *The Elements of a Child Care Licensing Statute: What to Look for in Your State's Law* (Boston, Mass.: Wheelock College, Center for Career Development in Early Care and Education, 1993), 3.

13. Gwen Morgan and Bettina McGimsey, *States' Policies on Qualifications for Roles in Early Care and Education: A Working Paper,* (Boston, Mass.: Wheelock College, Center for Career Development in Early Care and Education 1993), 1.

14. Gwen Morgan, *The Facts of Life: How Child Care Licensing Requirements Are Created* (Boston, Mass.: Wheelock College, Center for Career Development in Early Care and Education, 1993), 5.

15. Nancy Rhyme, *Legislative Review of Administrative Rules and Regulations* (Denver, Colo.: National Conference of State Legislatures, August 1990).

16. W. T. Gormley, "Regulating Mister Rogers' Neighborhood: The Dilemmas of Day Care Regulation," *The Brookings Review* (Fall 1990): 24.

17. Adams, *Who Knows How Safe?*, vi.

18. 1991 Va. Acts, Chap. 595; 1993 Va. Acts, Chap. 730.

19. 1993 Nev. Stats., Chap. 299.

20. 1991 Md. Laws, Chap. 383.

21. 1991 Md. Laws, Chap. 321.

22. 1992 Md. Laws, Chap. 50.

23. 1991 Ohio Laws, H. 155.

24. 1990 N.Y. Laws, Chap. 750.

25. 1989 Tenn. Pub. Acts, Chap. 132.

26. Gnezda and Smith, *Child Care and Early Childhood Education Policy,* 3.

27. 1993 N.C. Sess. Laws, Chap. 321, Sec. 254.

28. 1991 Fla. Laws, Chaps. 266 and 300.

29. Children's Foundation, *1996 Family Child Care Licensing Study* (Washington, D.C.: Children's Foundation, 1996).

30. Children's Foundation, *1995 Family Child Care Licensing Study* (Washington, D.C.: Children's Foundation, 1995).

31. Children's Foundation, *1996 Family Child Care Licensing Study* (Washington, D.C.: Children's Foundation, 1996).

32. National Conference of State Legislatures, *State Legislative Summary: Children, Youth and Family Issues* (Denver: NCSL, 1991-96).

33. 1992 Ky. Acts, Chap. 57, Sec. 4.

34. 1993 Idaho Sess. Laws, Chap. 416.

35. 1992 Cal. Stats., Chap. 35.

36. 1991 Cal. Stats., Chap. 826.

37. Child Care Employee Project, *What States Can Do* (Oakland, Calif.: Child Care Employee Project, 1991), 9.

38. 1990 Va. Acts, Chap. 450.

39. 1993 Pa. Laws, Act 73.

40. Whitebook, Howes and Phillips, *Who Cares?*

41. Child Care Employee Project, "The National Child Care Staffing Study, 1992 Highlights of Major Findings and Recommendations," fact sheet (Oakland, Calif.: Child Care Employee Project, 1993).

42. Adams, *Who Knows How Safe?*, 56.

43. 1993 N.C. Laws, Chap. 561.

44. 1993 Me. Laws, Chap. 158.

45. Virginia Guzman, U.S. Department of Labor, Bureau of Labor Statistics, December 13, 1994: telephone conversation.

46. 1996 Fla. Laws, Chap. 175, Sec. 78.

47. National Center for Missing And Exploited Children, *State Criminal History Background Check Laws—Amendments and New Laws, 1995 Session* (Arlington, Va.,: NCMEC, 1995).

48. National Center for Missing and Exploited Children, *Selected State Legislation: A Guide for Effective State Laws to Protect Children, 3rd. ed.* (Arlington, Va.: National Center for Missing and Exploited Children, May 1993), 35, 48-53.

49. 1994 N.J. Laws, Chap. 350.

50. Children's Foundation, *1996 Child Day Care Licensing Study.*

51. 1991 Cal. Stats., Chap. 660; Patty Siegel, *Trustline and California's Registration Process for License Exempt Child Care Providers* (San Francisco, Calif.: California Child Care Resource and Referral Network, December 2, 1993).

52. 1991 Va. Acts, Chap. 595.

53. 1994 Iowa Acts, Chap. 1156.

54. U.S. General Accounting Office, *Child Care: States Face Difficulties Enforcing Standards and Promoting Quality* (Washington, D.C., November 1992), 3.

55. Helen Blank, *Protecting Our Children: State and Federal Policies for Exempt Child Care Settings* (Washington, D.C. Children's Defense Fund, January 1994), 14.

56. U.S. General Accounting Office, *Child Care: States Face Difficulties Enforcing Standards and Promoting Quality,* 4.

57. Ibid., 6.

58. "Care and Licensing Poor, OIG Finds," *Day Care USA,* February 7, 1994, 6-7.

59. U.S. General Accounting Office, *Child Care: States Face Difficulties Enforcing Standards and Promoting Quality,* 5.

60. 1990 Fla. Laws, Chap. 306, Sec. 37.

61. 1993 Tex. Gen. Laws, Chap. 977.

62. Helen Blank, *Investing In Our Care,* Table 1 (Washington, D.C.: Children's Defense Fund, June 1993).

63. National Association for the Education of Young Children, "Accreditation Criteria and Procedures of the National Academy of Early Childhood Programs," revised ed. (Washington, D.C.: NAEYC, 1991).

64. 1993 Me. Laws, Chap. 158; 1991 Ohio Laws, H. 155; 1994 Vt. Budget Bill, Sec. 138.

Chapter 7

1. U.S. General Accounting Office. *Child Care Subsidies Increase Likelihood that Low-Income Mothers Will Work,* Washington, D.C., December 1994.

2. Deborah Phillips and Anne Bridgman, eds., *New Findings on Children, Families, and Economic Self-Sufficiency: Summary of a Research Briefing,* (Washington, D.C.: National Academy Press, 1995).

3. Minneapolis Day Care Association, *Valuing Families: The High Cost of Waiting for Child Care Sliding Fee Assistance,* 1995.

4. Gary Seigel and Anthony Loman, *Child Care and AFDC Recipients in Illinois,* (Springfield, Ill.: Illinois Department of Public Aid, 1991).

5. Bruce Hershfield, Child Welfare League of America, testimony presented to the U.S. House Subcommittee on Human Resources, September 20, 1994, 5.

6. U. S. General Accounting Office, *Employment Training: Successful Projects Share Common Strategy,* Washington, D.C., May 1996, 11.

7. U. S. General Accounting Office, *Child Care: Working Poor and Welfare Recipients Face Service Gaps,* Washington, D.C., May 1994, 5.

8. Census Bureau, *Current Population Reports,* P70-52, Washington, D.C., September 1995.

9. Child Trends, Inc. *"How Well Are They Faring?"* Unpublished paper, Washington, D.C., 1-2.

10. Hershfield, testimony, 5.

11. Schweinhart, Barnes and Weikart, <u>Significant Benefits</u>, xvii, 55, 59-60, 91, 97, 106.

12. Bruner, Charles. *Child and Family Policy Center,* November 1996: Fax Communication.

13. Administration for Children and Families, *Characteristics and Financial Circumstances of AFDC Recipients: Fiscal Year 1995* (Washington, D.C., 1995).

14. Ibid., 15.

15. Ibid., 28.

16. Ibid., 1.

17. U.S. General Accounting Office, *Families on Welfare: Sharp Rise in Never Married Women Reflects Social Trend,* Washington, D.C., May 1994, 2.

18. Administration for Children and Families, 3, 11, and 18.

19. Maria Cancian and Daniel R. Meyer, *A Profile of the AFDC caseload in Wisconsin: Implications for a Work-Based Welfare Reform Strategy* (University of Wisconsin-Madison: Institute for Research on Poverty, 1995), 4-7.

20. Calculation based on figures from the *1996 Green Book,* United States House of Representatives, Committee on Ways and Means, Tables 1-17, 1-19 and A-25.

21. LaDonna Pavetti, *Time on Welfare and Welfare Dependency,* testimony for the House of Representatives, Committee on Ways and Means, Subcommittee on Human Resources, 104th Congress, May 3, 1996.

22. National Commission on Children, *Beyond Rhetoric: A New American Agenda For Children and Families,* final report (Washington, D.C., 1991), 40-41.

23. Administration for Children and Families, 13.

24. Mark Greenberg, Center for Law and Social Policy, October 1994: fax communication.

25. Jack Tweedie and Dana Reichert, *1996 Benefit Level Survey,* National Conference of State Legislatures, December 1995.

26. "The Health and Human Services Poverty Guidelines for 1996," URL= http://aspe.os.dhhs.gov/poverty/poverty.htm.

27. Tweedie and Reichert, Calculation using *1996 Benefit Level Survey, National Conference of State Legislatures,* 1996; and *1994 Green Book,* US House of Representatives, Committee on Ways and Means.

28. Administration for Children and Families, 44.

29. Furkas, Steve et al, "The Values We Live By: What Americans Want From Welfare Reform," *Public Agenda,* (New York, New York, 1996), 7, 9, 18.

30. Jack Tweedie and Dana Reichert, "Requiring Welfare Recipients to Work, " *LegisBrief* (National Conference of State Legislatures) 4, no. 48 (November/December 1996).

31. Children's Defense Fund, *State Early Care and Education Developments: 1995.*

32. 1996 Iowa Acts, Chap. 1213, Sec. 6 and 1995 Iowa Acts, Chap. 205, Sec. 6.

33. Children's Defense Fund, *Summary of Trends in State Early Care and Education Developments: 1996,* (Washington, D.C.: CDF, 1996).

34. Dana Reichert, "State Welfare Reform Provisions," National Conference of State Legislatures, October 1996.

35. Steve Savner and Mark Greenberg, *The CLASP Guide to Welfare Waivers: 1992-1995* (Washington, D.C., Center for Law and Social Policy, 1995), 40; Scott Groginsky, "Child Care and the Transition Off Welfare," *LegisBrief* (National Conference of State Legislatures) 4, no. 14 (March 1996).

36. University of Colorado at Denver, "Cost, Quality And Child Outcomes in Child Care Centers," *Public Report, 2nd ed.* (Denver: Economics Department, University of Colorado at Denver, 1995), 26.

37. Deborah Phillips and Anne Bridgman, eds. *New Findings on Children, Families, and Economic Self-Sufficiency: Summary of A Research Briefing,* (Washington, D.C., National Academy Press, 1995), 18.

38. Nancy Ebb, *Child Care and Welfare Reform: More Painful Choices,* (Washington, D.C.: Children's Defense Fund, 1995), 5.

39. Ellen Galinsky, et al., *The Study of Children in Family Child Care and Relative Care.* New York: Families and Work Institute, 1994.

40. *Working For Change* "Recruiting Welfare Recipients For Child Care Work: Not a Panacaea." San Francisco: Child Care Law Center, 1996.

41. 1996 Colo. Sess. Laws, Chap. 221.

42. LaDonna A. Pavetti and Amy-Ellen Duke, *Increasing Participation in Work and Work-Related Activities: Lessons Form Five State Welfare Reform Demonstration Projects, Final Report,* (Washington, D.C.,: The Urban Institute, 1995), 61.

43. Ann Shafer, Mississippi Department of Human Services, fax communication, December 4, 1996; and Mary Chamberlain, Texas Work Force Commission, December 4, 1996: telephone conversation.

44. LaDonna A. Pavetti and Amy-Ellen Duke, *State Welfare Reform Efforts, Executive Summary,* (Washington, D.C.: Urban Institute, 1996), 2.

45. Judith Havemann and Barbara Vobjeda, Washington Post. December 13, 1996. p.2.

46. Dave Lesher, "Oregon in the Spotlight as Welfare Reform Laboratory," *LA Times,* 12/19/96.

47. Jack Tweedie, "Welfare: What's Next?" *State Legislatures* (National Conference of State Legislatures) 23 no. 1 (January 1997): 20-24. Ron Snell and Arturo Perez, *State Budget Actions, 1996.* (Denver: National Conference of State Legislatures, 1996), 28-9.

48. Congressional Budget Office, "Total Costs to Meet Work Requirements Under H.R. 3734 as Passed By Congress." Congressional Budget Office, August 14,1996. Memorandum.

49. As enacted, states can only transfer TANF funds to the Social Services Block Grant by also transferring funds to the CCDBG. Up to 30 percent of TANF funds can be transferred to CCDBG and up to 10 percent of the 30 percent can then be transferred to the SSBG.

50. Congressional Budget Office, August 14,1996. Memorandum.

51. Helen Blank, Children's Defense Fund, November 27, 1996: telephone conversation.

52. U.S. Department of Health and Human Services, Administration of Children and Families, Child Care Bureau, *Principles for Planning,* (Washington, D.C.: 1996).

53. 1996 Fla. Laws, Chap. 175, Sec. 85; Sean Lewis, *A Summary of Provisions of New Child Care Laws in the State of Florida,* Florida House of Representatives Aging and Human Services Committee (Tallahassee, Fla.: 1996), 2.

54. State of Colorado, *Report of the Colorado Business Commission on Child Care Financing,* (Denver, CO: December 1995).

55. Sam Williams, Colorado Office of Business Development, December 4, 1996: telephone conversation; State of Colorado, *Report of the Colorado Business Commission on Child Care Financing,* (Denver, CO: December 1995).

56. Nancy Ebb, *Child Care and Welfare Reform.*

57. Congressional Budget Office, Memorandum.

58. University of Colorado at Denver, *Public Report,* 71.

59. U.S. Department of Health and Human Services, *Principles for Planning.*

60. "Helping Families Work: Alternatives To The Child Care Disregard," in *Working For Change* (San Francisco, Calif.: The Child Care Law Center, August 1994), 5, 7.

61. Ibid., 13, 20.

62. Ibid., 12-13.

63. Michele Piel, Illinois Department of Public Aid, September 27, 1994: telephone conversation.

64. Rhonda Present, Chicago JOBS Council, May 30, 1996: telephone conversation.

65. "Illinois: Irregular Work Hours and Child Care Needs," *CLASP Update* (CLASP, Washington, D.C.), July 2, 1996, 20.

66. Michele Piel, Illinois Department of Public Aid, November 13, 1996: telephone conversation.

67. Ibid.

68. Dianna Gordon, "The Welfare Monster," *State Legislatures* (National Conference of State Legislatures) 20, no. 6 (June 1994): 21.

69. 1993 Iowa Acts, Chap. 172, Sec. 42.

70. Iowa Department of Human Services, "Summary of Mathematica Policy Research, Inc." *Annual Reports On The Evaluation of Iowa's Welfare Reform,* (Des Moines, IA: February 5, 1996).

71. 1995 Iowa Acts, Chap. 205, Sec. 6; 1996 Iowa Acts, Chap. 1213, Sec. 6.

72. 1996 Iowa Acts, Chap. 1213, Sec. 6.

73. Don Kassar, Iowa Department of Human Services November 13, 1996: telephone conversation.

74. Catherine Alter and Jan L. Losby, *Evaluation of Iowa's FaDSS Program: A Family Support Program for Long-Term Welfare Recipients,* (Iowa City, IA: Institute for Social and Economic Development, 1995), iii-vi.

75. Cathie Pappas, Utah Department of Human Services, November 13, 1996: telephone conversation.

76. 1996 Utah Laws, Chap. 147, Sec. 16.

77. John Davenport, Utah Department of Human Services, November 13, 1996: telephone conversation.

78. Ibid.

79. Bureau of the Census, *1996 Current Population Survey.*

80. "The Health and Human Services Poverty Guidelines for 1996," URL=http://aspe.os.dhhs.gov/poverty/poverty.htm.

81. U.S. General Accounting Office, *Child Care: Working Poor and Welfare Recipients Face Service Gaps,* Washington, D.C.

82. 1993 N.J. Laws, Chap. 46.

83. 1992 Ky. Acts, Chap. 57, Sec. 8.

84. 1993 Cal. Stats., Chap. 1296.

85. 1993 Me. Laws, Chap. 158.

86. 1991 Ohio Laws, H. 155.

87. 1996 Fla. Laws, Chap. 175, Secs. 57-58, 78.

Chapter 8

1. Juliet B. Schor, *The Overworked American* (n.p.: BasicBooks, Harper Collins, 1991), 150.

2. Carnegie Task Force, *Starting Points,* 17, 18.

3. Schor, *The Overworked American,* 12.

4. Carollee Howes et al., "Thresholds of Quality: Implications for the Social Development of Children in Center-based Child Care, " *Child Development 63* (1992): 453-454.

5. Ellen Galinsky et al., *The Study of Children in Family Child Care and Relative Care, Highlights of Findings* (New York, N.Y.: Families and Work Institute, 1994), 4.

6. Whitebook, Howes and Phillips, *Who Cares?* 4.

7. Schor, *The Overworked American,* 1, 5, 29, 11-13.

8. Carnegie Task Force, *Starting Points*, 46.

9. National Commission on Children, *Beyond Rhetoric: A New American Agenda for Children and Families,* final report (Washington, D.C., 1991), 4-8, 137.

10. The National Center on Child Abuse Prevention Research, *Current Trends in child Abuse Reporting and Fatalities: The Results of the 1995 Annual Fifty State Survey* (Chicago: National Committee to Prevent Child Abuse, 1996).

11. Patrick A. Curtis et al., *Child Abuse and Neglect: A Look at the States—The CWLA Stat Book* (Washington, D.C.: Child Welfare League of America, 1995), 49.

12. National Commission on Children, *Beyond Rhetoric,* 284.

13. Shelley L. Smith, "Family Preservation and Support," *LegisBrief* (National Conference of State Legislatures) 2, no. 3 (January 1994).

14. Allen, Brown and Finlay, *Helping Children by Strengthening Families,* 39.

15. Ibid., 66.

16. Ibid., 51-53.

17. Catherine Alter and Jan L. Losby, *Evaluation of Iowa's FaDSS Program: A Family Support Program for Long-Term Welfare Recipients* (Iowa City: Institute for Social and Economic Development, 1995) iii-iv.

18. Research and Evaluation: "Kentucky Looks at the First Year of Its Statewide Program and Charts a Course for the Future," *Family Resource Coalition Report* 12, nos. 3 & 4, Family Support and School-Linked Services (Fall/Winter 1993): 47.

19. Faurest Coogle, "Schools With Youth Services Centers Associated With Improvement in Dropout Rates," *Kentucky School Advocate,* Kentucky School Boards Association, September 1996, 1, 4-5; John Kalafat, Robert J. Illback, Carryl Jeffries, *Implementation Evaluation of the Kentucky Family Resource and Youth Services Center Program: A Qualitative Analysis, Year Three* (Louisville, Ky.: R.E.A.C.H., 1995), 4-5.

20. Heather Weiss, *Pioneering States, Innovative Family Support and Education Programs,* 2nd ed. (Cambridge, Mass.: Harvard Family Research Project, 1992).

21. Robert Halpern and Heather Weiss, "Family Support and Education: Evidence from Evaluated Program Experience" (paper prepared for the 1990 Colloquium on Public Policy and Family Support, Family Resource Coalition, Chicago, April 1990).

22. *1994 Annual Report on Children's Initiatives,* Tennessee Select Committee on Children and Youth, June 9, 1994, 2, 6.

23. 1994 Tenn. Acts, Chap. 974, Sec. 6.

24. 1994 Vt. Acts, Act 154.

25. 1994 Wis. Laws, Act 444.

26. Legislative Research Commission, "Child Day Care Issues: Report to the 1993 General Assembly of North Carolina" (Raleigh, N.C., Legislative Library, January 1993).

27. 1993 N.C. Sess. Laws, Chap. 321, Sec. 254.

28. Mary Ellen Sylvester, North Carolina Legislative Fiscal Research Division, October 24, 1996: memo.

29. Ibid.

30. Coopers and Lybrand L.L.P., *State of North Carolina Smart Start Program Performance Audit, Final Report* (North Carolina: April 1996), 51-52.

31. 1994 N.C. Sess. Laws, Chap. 766.

32. Coopers and Lybrand L.L.P., *State of North Carolina Smart Start Program Performance Audit, Final Report* (North Carolina: April 1996), 51-52.

33. Mary Ellen Sylvester, memo.

34. North Carolina Department of Human Resources, "Smart Start" (April 1994, photocopy).

35. Mary Ellen Sylvester, memo.

36. Ibid.

37. Coopers and Lybrand, L.L.P., i, iv.

38. 1990 W.Va. Acts, Chap. 4, 3rd Extra Session.

39. Governor's Cabinet on Children and Families, *West Virginia's Family Resource Planning Fund: Construction of the Fund and Implementation in Year One,* May 15, 1996.

40. Barbara Merrill, West Virginia Cabinet on Children and Families, October 11, 1996: telephone conversation.

41. Steve Heasley, September 19, 1994: telephone conversation.

42. Steve Heasley, October 12, 1994: telephone conversation; Governor's Cabinet on Children and Families, "Operational Terms Related to Implementation: West Virginia Consolidated State Plan: (January 1994, photocopy).

43. Barbara Merrill, October 13, 1994: telephone conversation.

44. Barbara Merrill, September 16, 1994: telephone conversation.

45. Barbara Merrill, December 2, 1996: fax communication.

46. Barbara Merrill, October 25, 1996: telephone conversation.

47. Steve Heasley, September 19, 1994: telephone conversation.

43. Barbara Merrill, October 25, 1996: telephone conversation.

49. Family Resource Coalition, *Family Support Programs and School Readiness* rev. ed. (Chicago, Ill.: Family Resource Coalition, 1993).

ABOUT THE AUTHORS

Shelley L. Smith is the director of the Children and Families Program at the National Conference of State Legislatures which provides research, information, training, policy analysis, and technical assistance to state lawmakers on a broad range of issues. She co-authored of *A Legislators Guide to Comprehensive Juvenile Justice* and wrote *Family Preservation Services: State Legislative Initiatives* and numerous publications on state policy issues. Formerly with the Coalition for Family and Children's Services and the Iowa Commission on the Status of Women, she has served as a lobbyist, administered a program to remove children from adult jails, and managed campaigns at the state legislative level. She holds a masters degree in public administration from the University of Colorado and bachelor's degrees in journalism and mass communications and English from Iowa State University.

Mary Fairchild is a program principal in the Children and Families Program at the National Conference of State Legislatures (NCSL) in the area of juvenile justice and delinquency prevention. Previously, Ms. Fairchild was a private consultant specializing in human services policy and state legislative management and procedural issues for organizations including the NCSL, the National Center for State Courts, the City of Denver and private foundations. Ms. Fairchild previously worked in NCSL's criminal justice and legislative management programs. She holds a masters degree in social work from the University of Denver and a bachelor's degree in political science from Colorado State University.

Scott Groginsky is a policy specialist with the National Conference of State Legislatures' Children and Families Program. He coordinates the Early Childhood Care and Education Project that provides information services, legislative training sessions, and a variety of technical assistance to legislators interested in improving early childhood systems. He has written the issue briefs, *Child Care for Low-Income Families* and *Child Care and the Transition Off Welfare,* and co-authored the article, "An Ounce of Prevention" in NCSL's *State Legislatures* magazine. He received a bachelor of arts degree in political science from George Washington University in 1988.

Related Titles from the National Conference of State Legislatures

Early Childhood Care and Education: An Investment That Works
Revised edition with new chapter outlining recent federal laws on child care and welfare reform. Focuses on early childhood programs and how they affect the economy, education, juvenile violence and delinquency prevention, health, family support, and welfare. Written by Shelley Smith, Scott Groginsky, and Mary Fairchild. ©1997. ISBN 1-55516-650-4 Item #6137....**$25**

1996 State Legislative Summary: Children, Youth and Family Issues
Provides summaries of laws affecting children and families enacted in the 50 states and the District of Columbia during the 1996 legislative session. Topics include child abuse and neglect, child care and early childhood education, child support, custody and visitation, juvenile justice, welfare reform, youth-at-risk, family preservation, family support, financing and more. This reference also profiles legislative innovations, policy trends and major systems reform taking place across the nation. Produced by NCSL's Children and Families Program. ©1996. 124 pages ISBN 1-55516-605-9 Item #6136.... **$25**

1995 State Legislative Summary: Children, Youth and Family Issues
Provides summaries of laws affecting children and families enacted in the 50 states and the District of Columbia during the 1995 legislative sessions. Topics include child abuse and neglect, child care and early childhood education, child support, custody and visitation, juvenile justice, welfare reform, youth-at-risk, family preservation, family support, financing and more. This reference also profiles legislative innovations, policy trends and major systems reform taking place across the nation. Produced by NCSL's Children and Families Program. ©1995. 156 pages. ISBN 1-55516-607-5 Item #6135.... **$25**

A Legislator's Guide to Comprehensive Juvenile Justice
This guide is a must for anyone working on or affected by juvenile justice and prevention policies including: early childhood care and education, child protection, juvenile justice and violence prevention. Includes resources and trends. © 1996. Folder with 8 inserts. ISBN 1-55516-902-5 Item #9375....**$20**

- -

ORDER FORM

Title	Price	Quantity	Total

☐ **Please send me a FREE Publications Catalog**

SUBTOTAL	
SALES TAX (In Colorado 7.3%, in Washington, D.C. 6%)	
SHIPPING AND HANDLING (1st book $4.00, each additional book $1.00)	
FOR FEDERAL EXPRESS OVERNIGHT SERVICE (Add an additional $10.00 to shipping and handling)	
TOTAL AMOUNT DUE	

PLEASE PRINT OR TYPE:

Name_____ Title_____

Company_____

Address_____

City_____State_____ Zip _____

Phone (   ) _____ Method of Payment ☐ Visa   ☐ MasterCard   ☐ AmericanExpress

Credit Card Number _____ Exp. Date_____

Signature_____

FOR FASTEST SERVICE CALL OR FAX YOUR ORDER!

MAIL YOUR ORDER TO: **National Conference of State Legislatures**
Book Order Department
1560 Broadway, Suite 700
Denver, CO 80202
Federal ID #840772595

Phone
(303) 830-2054

FAX

(303) 863-8003